"When my daddy was seriously sick in 1918, my mother, together with the two oldest children, took over the farming duties. She is shown here driving the binder during harvest."

Road from Hilldene

Growing Up on a Farm in the Great Depression

LeROY DAY

PRIMIX
PUBLISHING
THE WRITE CHOICE

Primix Publishing
11620 Wilshire Blvd
Suite 900, West Wilshire Center, Los Angeles, CA, 90025
www.primixpublishing.com
Phone: 1-800-538-5788

Published by Primix Publishing: 02/13/2024

ISBN: 979-8-88703-216-0(sc)
ISBN: 979-8-88703-217-7(hc)
ISBN: 979-8-88703-218-4(e)

Library of Congress Control Number: 2023906109

For my children,
David, Jean, Michael
And
Grandchildren,
Stefan and Lauren

Contents

Acknowledgments

Grateful thanks to:

My mother, whose annotated picture album revived many memories; Latimer Watkins, my cousin, whose memories of my parents filled in many blanks; Barbara Wright, my niece, who supplied information on her father, my brother, Robert; Shirley Mounce, my sister Clara's daughter, who filled in forgotten details about her mother; Gretchen Harding, my niece, who helped me remember some of our childhood activities; Roberta Brunson and Karen Harris who supplied me with photographs of their fathers; Julian "Tweed" Cottrell and Greg Dinardi who generously took time to help me through problems with my computer; and Jackson Day, who allowed me to use excerpts from his book on the genealogy of the Day family.

Last, but not least, my wife, Mary, who gave me encouragement, helpful suggestions and performed the tedious task of editing the manuscript.

Life can only be understood backward.
But it must be lived forward.
— Kierkegaad

Prologue

The Great Depression started in the United States when the stock market crashed in 1929. This caused a loss of confidence in the economy which resulted in a sharp reduction in spending and investment. Bank closures followed and that led to widespread panic and layoff of workers. In summary, the economy contracted and many were suddenly jobless. Those in the cities were hit the hardest. Despite numerous government policies the Great Depression lasted for nearly 10 years.

"Road from Hilldene" is a true story of how one farming family coped with this period. Hilldene farm had no electricity, no radio, no powered farm equipment; all the farming was done with horse and mule. Transport was by horse and wagon. They planted a variety of crops that furnished food for both the animals as well as the family. Two cows furnished milk; chickens gave eggs and an occasional chicken dinner. Every Fall a young cow and a pig were butchered for meat. Vegetables, fruit and meat were preserved for winter. Wheat and corn were ground into flour and cornmeal at a nearby mill.

Under the poor economic conditions of the Depression, this family, not only survived, they demonstrated the value and joy of self-reliance.

That's a lesson which is applicable in our times as well.

Introduction

G rowing up as a child on a farm during the Great Depression was vastly different from the upbringing of my children and grandchildren in today's suburban environment. Things as they know them are so different that they can barely comprehend my early life. Vast changes have taken place in the seventy-plus years since I was a child. In addition to the material changes wrought by the rapidly advancing technology, our life styles and the social culture today bears little relationship to what I experienced as a child. This is the reason I wrote this book. Hopefully, it will help them understand and appreciate their family and ancestors.

The Appendix traces the line of our family back to 1720, the birthdate of John Day. It also lists my descendents, their spouses and children.

1

City Girl and Farm Boy

I never discussed with either my mother or father how a city girl from Richmond, Virginia, happened to meet and marry the son of a Kemptown, Maryland farmer. On the surface it always seemed to me to be an unlikely match of Sallie Caskie Lester and Ira Eugene Day. How did they get together? Long after both my parents died, I learned the story from my cousin, Latimer Watkins. My mother, Sallie C. Lester, was an excellent student. When she finished high school, she applied to Normal School for the training she would need as a teacher. She greatly admired her high school principal, Mr. Leroy Edwards, and asked him for a recommendation. In fact, she told me that she had chosen my first and middle names after Mr. Edwards. He wrote a letter of recommendation for her when she applied for a teacher's position.

Principal, Springfield School
Richmond, Virginia
Sep 12, 1900

To Whom it may concern,

Miss Sallie C. Lester was among the best pupils who has attended this school during the past eight (8) years. She was diligent in studies, courteous in deportment, ambitious to meet all the responsibilities of a pupil. Her success in this school was everyway satisfactory.

On entering High School she at once took high stand in her classes, completing the regular and postgraduate courses with high honors.

Miss Lester possesses those qualities of head and heart which eminently fit one for the work of teaching. I am sure that she will succeed in the profession.

Leroy S. Edwards
Principal

Sallie C. Lester, my mother. An excellent student, off to Normal School to become a teacher. Circa 1900.

Latimer W. and Venia Day, my grandparents. He was a
prosperous tobacco farmer of Kemptown, Maryland.

Mama, as all of us children called her, graduated from high school at age eighteen. After high school she attended Normal School. Soon thereafter, Sallie Caskie Lester began her career as a teacher. She had been teaching near Richmond, Virginia, for a couple years when one weekend a woman, who was a friend and also a teacher, invited Mama to visit her family in Maryland. My mother's friend was from the little town of Kemptown about fifteen miles southeast of Frederick, Maryland. Her father was the Reverend Cullom, Pastor of the Providence Methodist Protestant Church of Kemptown, which was built in 1836. This was where the Day family worshiped. It was at this church that Sallie Lester met Ira Day, son of Latimer and Venia Browning Day. Latimer Day was a prosperous tobacco farmer whose farm was just a few miles from Kemptown. Latimer and Venia Day had two children, Ira, and a daughter, Melissa. Ira was two years older than Sallie.

Following this chance meeting, Sallie and Ira had a short courtship and announced that they were to be married in Sallie's hometown, Richmond, Virginia on December 11, 1902. They were married at St. John's Protestant Episcopal Church, the Reverend R. A. Goodwin presiding. Mother was twenty-one years old and my father was twenty-three years old. Ira had worked on his father's farm all his life. In those days farming boys in Maryland were often referred to as "six graders." The sixth grade of grammar school was as far as most of them went. By that time they were old enough to be a substantial help on the farm and so they quit school. In some rare instances, if a boy was unusually talented, the teacher might persuade the family to allow him to go another year and finish the seventh grade. But that was it. Girls might actually go farther in school than boys as their labor was not so critically needed. In Mama's case, she had come from a well educated family. She had finished high school in Richmond, Virginia, with honors and then gone on to additional study to qualify her as a teacher. From there she had gone into teaching. So it was a union of two entirely different backgrounds and cultures—city girl and farm boy. But they were attracted to each other and were happily married.

After they were married, Mama and Daddy moved into a small house on Grandfather Day's farm. This house was only a hundred yards from the big farmhouse. Daddy continued working on the farm with his father as he had done all his life. The first child born was Janice, one and a half years after they were married. A son was born four years later and named Randolph. A second daughter, Thelma, was born in 1910. It was now getting crowded in that small house on Grandfather's farm. In addition, Mama found it a little confining to be living so close under the watchful eye of her mother-in-law. Their relationship was cordial but cool. No doubt Grandmother Day resented her farmer son marrying a young schoolteacher from a city in the South. In those days it was customary to marry someone from the same area and probably from a like culture. Farmers married farm girls and city girls married city men. Mama longed also to be closer to her family in Richmond. The little of town of Kemptown had nothing to compare to the city of

Richmond. Kemptown had a general store and post office combined, a grammar school and the Methodist Protestant Church. All social activities revolved around the church.

With three children, Mama became restless in the small house and living so close to her mother-in-law. Once the children were in bed, the talk of moving, so they could have a place of their own, became a regular topic of discussion between Mama and Daddy. Finally Mama took action and wrote to her brother, Page Lester, a dentist in Richmond, who also did a little real estate dealing. She asked him to try to locate a farm close to Richmond. Nearly a year later, Page wrote that he had finally found a 241 acre farm near the town of Doswell, twenty miles north of Richmond. This was hopeful news for Mama and Daddy. Of course, the scant description given by Mama's brother wasn't enough to tell if this farm would be satisfactory. Finally, it was time to break the news to the senior Days that Mama and Daddy were considering leaving Maryland for a farm in Virginia. Grandfather and Grandmother were understandably cool to the idea. Grandfather was very dependent on his farmer son who had worked with him all these years. Grandmother Day would certainly miss her son who had been close by for all his thirty-two years. Mama, who always managed the money in the family and knew their meager savings, wondered how they might swing the deal. And Daddy must have been apprehensive although he certainly knew all there was to know about farming. There was considerable discussion between the two sets of parents and finally they agreed that nothing could be decided until the farm was visited.

The Day family of Kemptown, Maryland. My father, mother and Janice, age 5, and Randolph, age 3. Circa 1909.

Daddy and Grandfather Day went down to Doswell by train in the summer of 1912 to have a look at the farm. The farm was two miles from the little town of Doswell down a winding dirt road through dense woods. There were no other houses on the road. About three quarters of the acreage was open land suitable for cultivation; the remainder was in timber, hardwood and pine. The two-story farmhouse had adequate room for a family. Just outside the kitchen of the farmhouse was a smokehouse for curing meat. There were a number of farm buildings, including a stable and several small buildings suitable for chickens. Unfortunately, there was not a barn for storing hay and grain as well as a place for the animals and farm equipment. Some of the other buildings would have to suffice until a barn could be built. This lack of a barn bothered both Grandfather and Daddy. They wondered how a farm could have been operated without a suitable barn. Well, they decided that was just something that would have to be solved if and when Daddy and Mama bought the farm.

The land had two levels. The house and all of the out buildings and most of the open land and the woods were on the upper level. A short distance east of the house the land sloped down to a level plain that was open for quite a distance and finally turned into a pine forest. Into the pine forest about 500 yards was the North Anna River. The eastern boundary of the farm was just a little into the pine forest. This lower level of land we called the "flats." It was sandy and a good place to grow watermelons, cantaloupes and strawberries. One section on the lower level below the out buildings became a pasture. On the sandy flats we later found many Indian arrowheads. It was told that the flats was a small lake at one time and that the Indians might have been shooting fish or waterfowl with bow and arrow. The Indians here would have been Pamunkey, a tribe of the Powatan Nation. (Pocahontas was also a Powatan from the area near Jamestown, Virginia, about 150 miles to the southeast.)

Grandfather and Daddy returned from the farm visit and pronounced it suitable. It had no really rich soil like "river bottom loam," but it would make a livable home. So the decision was to make the move from Maryland to the farm near Doswell, Virginia. Grandfather Day made a generous gift of $12,000 to Daddy to enable him to buy the farm. This was in consideration for the years Daddy had worked on Grandfather's farm.

By January 1913 the purchase of the farm was settled. It was bought from Mr. Doswell who owned much of the land around the town of Doswell. The town of Doswell was named for the Doswell family. Mama and Daddy began preparations to move from Kemptown. Mama had the three children to manage and she was pregnant with another as well. Janice was nine, Randolph was seven and Thelma was three. Grandmother Day agreed to accompany Mama and the children on the train from Frederick down to Doswell, a distance of a little over one hundred miles. Meanwhile, Daddy and Grandfather planned how they would transport some household items, two horses and a cow. There was no practical way but to drive a wagon and lead the cow. Grandfather had been generous again and gave Daddy two horses, a farm wagon and a milk cow. They made the trip in a little over a week. The horse drawn wagon was piled with furniture and household and personal items. The milk cow was led by a rope tied to the wagon tailgate. Once at the farm they began to set up house and then returned to Doswell to meet the train bringing Mama and the children and Grandmother Day. Grandfather and Grandmother stayed only a few days to help Mama and Daddy get settled and then returned by train to Maryland. This was the first time in eleven years that Mama and Daddy had been completely independent. This would be their home for the next twenty-six years and where they would raise eight children.

2

Depression Years

Hard Times and Hobos

The US stock market crashed in 1929 and the country was plunged into a deep depression that lasted a decade. In spite of the various government programs that President Roosevelt put into place, the country was still struggling until the build-up for World War II started in '39 - '40. I was born in January 1925 so my entire childhood was during the Depression. Millions were out of jobs and a certain hopelessness swept the country. Haircuts were fifteen cents and a day laborer was paid a dollar a day if he could find work. To some extent we were isolated from the worst effects of the Depression because we lived on a farm. We supplied most of our own food by our own labors and kept other expenses to a minimum by "doing without." That was one of my mother's expressions, "Well, I guess we will just have to do without." How many times did I hear her say that in response to some question of mine about something I wanted! As a child I never realized how bad things were, particularly in the cities. Of course, there were also farms that suffered terribly and many were abandoned, particularly in the Midwest, but I never realized it. My world was very limited, mostly to our farm, the nearby town of Doswell and the railroads, with an occasional visit to Richmond. I did know that we were better off than our immediate neighbors: the Cannons and the Mitchells. We never were hungry; we had warm clothes for winter, caring parents and a school for learning. There was plenty of work but also time for play. I had a happy childhood. Looking back I now know it must have been a worrisome time for Mama and Daddy. Sure, we had the basics for food: fresh meat from a hog or heifer we butchered in the fall, stored vegetables and fruits like potatoes, apples, cabbage, carrots, turnips which were kept in the cellar and all the meat, vegetables, and fruit which Mama canned. I remember the rows of glass Mason jars containing all these foods on the shelves in the cellar. We also had flour and cornmeal made from wheat and corn we had grown and taken to the mill on the South Anna River about seven miles away. But there were clothes to be bought for the growing children, certain necessary household items like kerosene for lamps and gasoline for the engines to pump water and saw wood. Also, we had to buy food items that we couldn't grow on the farm: coffee, tea, sugar and the like. Mama told me that plenty of times they were out of coffee and had no money to buy so they used dried soy beans ground to make a hot beverage. We really didn't have a "cash crop." We sold a few chickens and eggs to Campbell's General Store in Doswell. In the summer we sold vegetables and fruits to the Doswell townspeople. We also sold some pine logs to the mills in Doswell that made excelsior, a packing material. The end result was that there was very little cash. I know Mama sometimes got a check from her brother, Charlie, in Richmond. Mama was a frugal manager of what little money we had. At times it must have been harrowing for my parents.

Grandfather, Latimer W. Day, had a two-hundred acre farm that produced a profitable crop of tobacco every year. Tobacco was a labor intensive crop but the profits were worth it. Maryland couldn't grow the best type of tobacco because the climate wasn't ideal for tobacco. Even so, the farm produced a reliable cash crop every year. A much higher grade of tobacco was grown in Southern Maryland, Virginia and North Carolina. Having grown up on Grandfather's farm, Daddy knew all about raising tobacco. In fact, he continued to work on Grandfather's farm even after he and Mama were married while they lived in the "little house" on the farm. However, when he and Mama moved to their farm in Virginia, near Doswell, Mama said they would not raise tobacco. She didn't want her family brought up in what she called the "tobacco culture." Looking back I am glad she made that decision but it did influence what crops we had on the farm and probably resulted in us not having a real "cash crop." During the depression there was not much market where we lived to sell corn or wheat which were our two main crops. Our crops were pretty well diversified to provide food for the animals and also for that growing family.

*Some years we had good crops. Here is Daddy showing
Janice, (my oldest sister), a bumper crop of soybeans
which will feed the farm animals over the winter.*

Comes the end of August it was time to review the status of clothes for all of us children in time for school. Hand-me-downs were used as much as practical but Mama always wanted us to look decent for school. So, one night toward the end of summer, we would sit around the kitchen table and get out the Sears Roebuck catalog to place an order for those things we absolutely had to buy. Chances are that I had outgrown whatever I had worn the previous school year. Probably Mama would order a pair of gray or dark green corduroy knickers for me. For the cold weather I would need a new pair of leather lace-up boots. I always asked for the ones that had a pocket on the outside of the right boot for a pocket knife. Sometimes the pocket knife was included. What a special thrill. Unless I had a hand-me-down sweater from my brother, Emil, maybe I'd get a new sweater. Coats and jackets were always passed down so seldom would I get a new one. Being the youngest child I usually had a pretty good choice of clothes the others had outgrown. Nothing was thrown away.

One thing I remember about the Depression years was the prevalence of "hobos." These were men who were out of jobs or some were just homeless. Others were traveling to other locales in search of work. Although it was illegal, they rode the freight trains often stopping in Doswell to buy a can of beans or ask for a handout. Many times we would see three or four huddled around a fire in the edge of the woods along the road to our farm. They might be only a hundred yards from the last house in Doswell. There was little crime associated with the hobos. I am sure there were some who stole food but it was not common. People considered them a nuisance but understood the desperate situation they were in because everyone was suffering from the Depression in some way. Sometimes they would come to a house and ask if they could work for a meal: maybe a couple hours of splitting wood or some work in the garden. Our farm was two miles from the railroads down a winding dirt road so I can't remember anytime when a hobo came to our farm.

There was a certain adventuresome aspect to the idea of getting on a train and traveling to some far away place. Whenever I was in Doswell, and near to the railroads, I would read the names on the boxcars and imagine what those far away places were like: the Great Northern, Union Pacific, Burlington, Southern Pacific and others. My world was pretty local. Up until I was ten years old, I had only been the twenty miles to Richmond and once on the train with Mama to visit a lady friend in Washington. Once I also got to visit Grandfather and Grandmother Day in Kemptown, Maryland.

I loved to watch the trains going through Doswell. There was a signal tower at the intersection of the Chesapeake and Ohio (C and O) and Richmond, Fredericksburg and Potomac (RF&P) Railroads there in Doswell. Once I got permission to go up in the tower where they monitored and operated the signal lights and switches for these two railroads in the area near Doswell. From the tower you had a clear view down both tracks and could see a train coming a mile away. Inside the tower were banks of lights and levers that controlled the switches and warning lights along the tracks as the trains approached this crossing. There was also a telegraph operator who could signal other stations to give the status of trains passing through Doswell. These operators had a great responsibility to ensure that no two trains approached this crossing at the same time. There was never an accident while I lived on the farm and I never heard of one ever happening at this railroad crossing in Doswell. I marveled at the telegraph operators; they were so fast sending and receiving messages by code. One Christmas I got a toy telegraph station with two key stations, batteries and about a hundred feet of connecting wire. There was also a book of Morse code. I learned a little code and when my nephew and niece, Roger and Gretchen, were visiting from Richmond, we set up the two stations to play. We set one station in the house and other in the yard. We had a good time sending simple messages to each other. My brother, Emil, also played "telegraph" with me sometimes. About this time Emil moved to Richmond to finish high school and I was alone. It wasn't any fun learning code if there was no one to send the message to so my "telegraph operator" phase came to an end.

The trains that came through Doswell were an important transportation link to the outside world. If we wanted to go to Richmond, we went by train. If Daddy ordered fertilizer or lime for the farm, it came by train to the freight depot at Doswell. Mail came by train, too. And, as I mentioned earlier, the two main sources of jobs other than farming were the railroads and the two excelsior mills. The "through trains" going from Richmond to Washington kept a pretty good schedule. One train, No. 99, passed through Doswell without stopping on its way north to Washington. It gave a long mournful whistle as it passed through the town and we could hear it down on our farm nearly two miles away. Daddy would stop whatever he was doing and go into the kitchen and check the time on the kitchen clock over the table. "Old

99 is right on schedule. It's eight o'clock exactly. 'Bout time to go to bed. I have to get that corn planted while the weather is good."

Besides the hard work, farming was all about the weather. Listening to my parents discussing the weather it seemed it was either raining too much or raining too little. Making good crops was a delicate balance between the amount of rain and when it came. A wet spring delayed the planting and made for a poor crop. A lack of rain during the growing season meant stunted plants and a poor yield—another poor crop. Rain during the harvest could also ruin a crop. If rain came just after the hay was mowed in early summer, the hay would mildew and be lost. Little wonder that the conversation between farmers always began and ended with a comment or two about the weather. The last thing my Daddy did every night before going to bed was to go outside and try to assess what the weather would be the next day. "The wind is blowing up from the East and maybe we'll get a little rain tomorrow. If we don't get some pretty soon, my corn isn't going to be waist high this year."

I was seven years old in 1932 when the country suffered a severe drought. Things had been bad in 1930 with very little rain but 1932 was worse. In the mid west it was the beginning of the "Dust Bowl" years. After years of plowing and years of below rainfall, the hot winds simply churned up and blew away the topsoil. It was so dry that the plants never got a start before they withered up and died. It was a hopeless time for those Midwest farmers and thousands simply gave up and took what little belongings they had and headed west. There was a great mass migration to California. Meantime in the East, things were not much better. We had had a dry year in 1930 and struggled through with poor yields on our crops. The wheat didn't fully develop and the few ears of corn on each stalk were small and missing most of the kernels. So 1930 had given us a taste of drought but the worst was yet to come.

The September 25, 1932 issue of the Richmond Times-Dispatch newspaper was headlined:

"Drought More Serious Than in 1930." The headline was followed by: "Officials Show Acute Distress of Population. Crops are Wiped Out as Months Pass with Rainfall at Minimum. Many Need Help. Reconstruction Finance Corporation Aid Is Sought to Aid Fully 500 Families." The lead story

went on to describe the failed crops and the desperate situation of farmers. This was a time when those on farms were worse off than their city neighbors.

On our farm, things became pretty hard because of the drought. The wheat that year was short and the grain heads were small. Of course, the wheat had been planted in the winter or early spring so it had at least gotten a start with the little spring rain. I remember some conversation between Mama and Daddy about whether it was going to be worth paying for the threshing machine operator to come that year. But we had to have the grain for our flour and feed for the chickens. I was interested in this discussion because the event of the threshing machine coming to our farm was a big thing for me; it broke up the monotony. At the age of seven I mostly had the fun of watching the whole operation. It wasn't until I was a bit older that I had to help with all of that hard, dirty work. Even then, I always looked forward to threshing time.

The summer crops were the hardest hit. The vegetable garden didn't yield many tomatoes, sweet corn, cucumbers, squash or other vegetables. The strawberries were marble size and pretty sour. The watermelon patch was mostly withered vines with a few scattered "head sized" melons and cantaloupes didn't mature at all. Both watermelons and cantaloupes require a lot of rain.

Probably the most serious crop loss was our corn because it was a primary food for the animals, the source of our cornmeal and the seed corn for next year's planting. The lack of rain had really stunted the corn. I was seven that summer and the corn never got as tall as I was. I remember walking with Mama and Daddy down some of the corn rows and hearing their comments, " Look at those puny little ears. Why a goat wouldn't even eat them! There's gonna be a pitiful harvest this year. It's hardly going to be worth taking this sorry corn down to the mill for grinding. I don't know what we're going to do."

Well, we did what Mama said so often we had to do, "I guess we'll just have to do without." I was too young to fully appreciate how bad things really were, but I know it was a time of terrible worrying for Mama and Daddy as they struggled to feed the family, the animals and keep the farm going. I know these hard times had a lot to do with the decisions of my brothers and sisters to leave the farm as soon as they graduated from high school and go to Richmond for a paying job.

Other Hard Times

I can hardly ever remember my Mama or Daddy being sick. I am sure if either one of them had been sick they would not mention it and would go about their work as best as they could. After all, there was work that had to be done. Of course, when the older children were home they did help out in such times.

Before I was born, during World War I , there was a time when Daddy was very sick for some time and Mama and the older children had to do essentially all the work on the farm. Possibly, Daddy was sick with that terrible Spanish influenza which was a worldwide epidemic, called a pandemic. It struck twice over two years, beginning in 1918. Some speculated that it had originated in China. It first appeared in this country in a military camp in Kansas, early in 1918. Then, as American troops and war materiel flooded the East Coast ports on their way to the war in Europe, there were further breakouts. By the time of the end of World War I, in November 1918, the scourge had spread to many countries around the world. A second wave of the influenza occurred in 1919 when all the troops returned to their homeland. It was particularly deadly for people who were 20 to 40 years old. It has been recorded as one of the world's greatest calamities and killed between 20 and 40 million people worldwide. It was estimated that the influenza killed over 600,000 people in the US, more that ten times the number of American soldiers killed in the war.

During this time while Daddy was sick, Mama had to run the farm. My oldest sister, Janice, was 13 at the time and old enough to do a lot of the housework as well as look after three younger children. Mama and my brother, Randolph, age 10, did the farm work. Mama's work came to the attention of the Hanover County Agent, Mr. J. C. Stiles, who wrote to Mr. H. C. Stuart, Governor of Virginia. Mr. Stiles' letter was published in the Richmond Times Dispatch.

"There is one farm in Hanover County owned and operated by Mr. and Mrs. I. E. Day of Doswell. They have about 150 acres under cultivation. There are five children in the family, the eldest being a girl of thirteen and a boy of ten. The boy belongs to the corn club and the girl to the poultry club. Mr. Day has only been able to hire three days of help on his farm this summer. He has tried hard to find help, but has been unable to do so.

Mrs. Day—a woman of about thirty-five years, born and raised in Richmond, a graduate of Richmond Normal School, and school teacher for several years—works in the field a large part of the time while the thirteen year old girl keeps house and takes care of the younger children. Mrs. Day has this season broken eighteen acres of land with a three-horse riding plow, cut six or eight acres of hay with a mowing machine and thirty acres of grain with a binder—a four-horse binder, with the ten year old boy on the lead horse. She has also driven the harrow over a large part of the fields, now in soy beans, peas and corn. For about two weeks the boy was rather sick with malaria, when the girl helped in the field with her mother. Mr. Day has been handicapped this season, since he has no help but his family, and he has a sawmill on his place cutting lumber for a barn and silo. He and the boy have logged the mill in addition to their duties on the farm.

They have grown on this farm this year 9 ½ acres of wheat, 15 ½ acres of rye, 5 acres of oats, 4 acres of oat hay, 17 acres of corn, 5 acres of soy beans, 12 acres of peas, 1 ½ acres of potatoes. They plan to sow 20 acres of wheat and 7 acres of oats and 45 acres of rye.

Our Women's Service leagues and our women who spend their time in sleeping, dressing and pleasure seeking might get some points from this lady."

The Times Dispatch also reported that:

"The Governor Stuart immediately wrote Mrs. Day a letter in which he said among other things:

'" I am in receipt of a letter from Mr. J. C. Stiles, county agent for Hanover County, in which he gives me a most interesting and noteworthy account of the results of your working on the farm. I wish to congratulate you and your family, not omitting, of course, Mr. Day, on this splendid spirit of determination and resourcefulness under difficulties.'"

A week later the Times Dispatch published a letter which Mama wrote back to Governor Stuart in response to his request for further particulars:

"We are still on the job. There are one or two days in the week that I remain at the house to do cleaning and baking and mending and then the boy and the girl take turns with the team, either harrowing or plowing. They do their work well and show an interest in it, much more than a hired hand.

At one time Mr. Day was taken sick, and with no help at all I was in a serious situation, but the boy and I put ourselves to the plows and we came out all right. We wanted to break about five, maybe six acres to sow in soja beans and at the time knew it could not wait. So we both went in the field and kept right at it. In good time we plowed and planted it all right, besides doing several other important jobs between times. I wish to say that it is a mistaken idea that it is a disgrace for a woman to go in the field. When there is a need of it and the necessity comes, it is most beautiful work and it is healthful, too, for my health has been better this summer than ever before."

The Times Dispatch continued by saying:

"Mrs. Day was unstinted in her praise of the children and their part in the good work of overcoming the difficulties of the scarcity of labor. Truly that scarcity is no bugbear to people like the Days, of Hildene Farm."

Mama was 43 years old when I was born, the youngest of her eight children. By the time I could remember anything about her she was in her late forties. I always remember how hard she worked in the house and how unselfish she was about doing things for all of us and our friends. However, it is remarkable to read about the amount of hard physical farm work she did when she was in her thirties. Besides Janice and Randolph, the two older ones, she also had Thelma, Clara and three-year old Robert at that time to look after. It is clear from her letter to the Governor of Virginia that she enjoyed the outside work and felt a strong sense of accomplishment. That wonderful sense of tackling a necessary job with determination and good humor was a trait of Mama's that I remember well.

3

Doswell

Doswell was a small town of less than a hundred people, not counting those that lived on the surrounding farms. It had a long history extending back before the Civil War. In those days it was known as Hanover Junction: Hanover for the county and Junction for the two railroads that crossed at Doswell. The two railroads were the Richmond, Fredericksburg and Potomac Railroad and the Chesapeake and Ohio Railroad. They were known respectively as the RF&P and the C&O railroads. The RF&P ran north and south connecting Richmond, Washington and New York. The C&O ran generally east and west connecting the eastern part of Virginia with points farther west. Doswell was also well situated for automobile and truck traffic because it was twenty miles north of Richmond just off of US #1 Highway which ran from Florida to Maine.

The town had a single paved road that wandered through the town crossing the two railroads and passing by Campbell's General Store and Allen's Store and Post Office and connecting to US #1 highway. The houses in Doswell were well kept; there were no "falling down" shacks. In fact, several of the houses along Doswell's "main street" were large impressive ones reflecting a more prosperous past. There was only one church in town, St. Martin's Episcopal Church, nestled close to the C&O tracks across from Allen's Store. Campbell's Store was the principal place of business; they had everything from food to shoes, tools, clothing and the only gasoline pump in town. It was truly a "general store." At any time there was usually a car or two and a horse and wagon parked outside. Just across the road from the store was a two story brick building that housed the bank. Mr. Oliver ran the bank and his family lived upstairs over the bank. His son, George Brown Oliver, and I were in the same class at school. We competed throughout our years in elementary school. We were friends though from an entirely different social strata. He was the son of the town banker; I was a freckled face farm boy from down the road. We both did well in our studies and it gave me special satisfaction when I "bested" him on a test or paper.

Now, Allen's Store was at the other end of town just across the C&O tracks. It was first a post office and secondarily a store. Allen's Store was primarily a food store without the wide assortment of things available at Campbell's. Of course, everybody had to go to Allen's Store for their mail which brought him some business, too. The Doswell Elementary School was only about two hundred yards from where the main road through the town connected to US #1 highway. The school building was a one story brick building with classrooms for seven grades. My brothers and sisters had gone to this same school. The student body was probably less than one hundred. My walking route home from school always took me by Allen's Store where I stopped to pick up the mail. I usually had a couple of boys to walk with until I entered the dirt road leading to our farm. The walk from school to our farm was about two miles.

The economy of Doswell was dependent mostly on two industries: the excelsior mills and the railroads. Of course, there was the retail business of the two stores and the bank. There was also a lumber mill just west of Doswell off of US #1. The excelsior mills bought pine logs from the surrounding area and turned them into the thread-like packing material called excelsior. The two railroad lines crossing in Doswell handled both passenger and freight traffic. There were at least a couple of passenger trains each day and numerous freight trains. There was a passenger depot right at the junction of the RF&P and C&O tracks. It was convenient no matter which train you were boarding or meeting. A quarter mile away was a freight terminal on a siding which also provided a way for freight cars to be transferred from one railroad to the other.

The town of Doswell got its name from the Doswell family. The Doswell family traced its history back to the Revolutionary War. The Doswell farm, or rather estate, was called Bullfield, about two miles east of the town of Doswell. In the early days, it was famous for breeding race horses and regularly held races at Bullfield. The peak of breeding and racing horses at Bullfield was from the 1890's into the early 1900's. The races were popular and brought crowds of people by train from Richmond. In fact, it was said that the building that housed Campbell's store was originally a "hotel" built for those who came to see the races at Bullfield. An article from the Richmond News Leader, published sometime in the '30's, tells of the race horse activity at Bullfield.

HorsesBy W. J. Carter

Back in 1891 Thomas Bernard Doswell, of Bullfield Farm, in Hanover County, then the oldest of Virginia breeding establishments, now a memory of the past, attended an auction in New York, and for a single bid of $100 secured a yearling colt, dejected in appearance and lacking individual excellence, though of attactive breeding. He was a son of Eolus, a great sire, and Cerise, daughter of Moccasin and Lizzie Lucas, a famous race mare of her day.

Wintered in Virginia and named Morello, ungainly as a yearling he was taken to the races at two years old and carrying on brilliantly from spring until autumn, the son of Eolus scored fourteen times first and achieved lasting fame as winner of the Futurity, while at three and four his name was carved in the top niche of fame as one of greatest race horses of all times.

In 1913 my parents bought our farm, Hilldene, which adjoined Bullfield. By that time the era of horse racing at Bullfield had passed, but I well remember people talking about the fact that there had been a race track down on the flats below our house.

As a boy I was not aware of the history of the Doswell area in the Civil War period. I did, however, find the remains of a Civil War pistol and many lead bullets on our farm. There were also the remnants of trenches in the woods on the western edge of our farm. It turns out that Doswell, known as Hanover Junction in the Civil War era, was several times the objective of Union forces who wanted to cut the rail lines supplying the Confederate forces. In the winter of 1863, while General Robert E. Lee was camped south of Fredericksburg with his Army of Northern Virginia, almost all of the supplies were brought north over the RF&P railroad. In an attempt to cut this supply line, Union forces under General Joe Hooker planned to circle west of Fredericksburg and destroy the rail lines at Hanover Junction. However, he was not successful and the rail lines were available to supply General Lee throughout that terrible winter. The food shortage was severe that winter for both the troops and their horses. Lee gave orders that the horses were to be shipped south on the railroad to Hanover Junction where good grazing was available. That was done and the horses remained in and around Hanover Junction until the worst of the winter was over. They were returned north by train.

There was a real Civil War battle that took place just a few miles north of Doswell/Hanover Junction near where the US #1 highway now crosses the North Anna River. The crossing in those days was named the Telegraph Road Bridge. The time was May 23-26, 1864. General Grant was continuing his offensive against Lee's Army of Northern Virginia and he hoped to cross the North Anna River and continue on his drive toward Richmond, twenty miles to the south. However, he was stopped by the placement of Lee's troops and forced to divide his army into three parts to attack. What followed was three days of bloody see-saw fighting. Lee planned to strike an offensive blow but he was sick and the chance was lost. Once Grant discovered the full threat of Lee's forces, he withdrew back across the North Anna River and then proceeded southeast on toward Richmond. The battle was indecisive although Lee had prevented Grant from advancing across the North Anna at this point. The estimated casualties were 4,000.

Because fighting took place at different points along the river over the three days, several names are used for the battles: Telegraph Road Bridge, Jericho Mill, Ox Ford, Quarles Mill and Hanover Junction.[1]

On US #1 Highway, near the North Anna crossing, there was a house which Mama said was called the "cannon ball" house because of a hole near the front door from an errant cannon shot in the Civil War. No doubt this occurred during the battle along the North Anna River just described.

The little town of Doswell was my first encounter with society outside of our family. I started school there; I bought things at the two stores; I had some classmate friends in Doswell; I had my first "paying job" cutting grass for Mrs. Myers who lived next to Campbell's Store and together with my brother, Emil, we sold fruit and vegetables door to door from our farm wagon. As a boy, Mama took me to Richmond sometimes by train from Doswell. For me, it always represented a departure point to the greater outside world.

4

Our Farmhouse

When Mama and Daddy moved to the farm in 1913, it had a two story house as shown in old photographs. Later, they modified it to a one story with a sort of half room at the head of the stairs which came up from the hall near the living room. That space upstairs had a half wall and space for a single bed and a small chest of drawers. It was the bedroom for boys and I had it after my brothers. I remember the wallpaper featured cowboys, horses and cows. I used to lie in bed and fantasize about being a cowboy. It was really a "space", not a room. I always liked it because of the privacy. It was separated from the family because it was on the upper level. It also had a dormer window that looked out on our yard and the fields beyond. From this sleeping space there was a door leading into the attic. The attic was our secret playing place we used whenever my nieces, Gretchen and Evelyn, and nephew, Roger, were up visiting from Richmond. You could stand up in the center portion of the attic. The attic also contained a large circular tank that provided water for the bath and kitchen, which was quite a luxury for a farmhouse in those days. Certainly, none of our neighbors had anything like that. The tank was round and open at the top—like a half barrel. It was made of wood staves just like a barrel and stood about three feet high. Our well was about 75 yards from the house and water was pumped by a small gas engine.

Our house had a living room with fireplace and also the main register over a wood-burning furnace in the cellar. We had a dirt cellar, not a regular basement. One part of the cellar was for the furnace; another section was storage for apples, potatoes, other root vegetables and most of Mama's canned food. I still remember the musky smell mixed with the aroma of apples that greeted you when you entered the cellar.

Besides the living room, there was the kitchen and three bedrooms. When all of my brothers and sisters had left the farm, the third bedroom became a dining room. The central item in the kitchen was a large black iron wood stove. It was an important source of heat and where Mama cooked all our meals. There were three warm places in our house in the winter: over that register in the living room, the living room fireplace and the kitchen. The furnace had pipes connected to each of the bedrooms but very little heat ever came out. Of course, there was no blower because we had no electricity. High voltage transmission lines ran right through our farm on the slope just below the barn. But there were no other houses close by that would justify a substation so we never had any electricity as long as I lived on the farm. At bedtime we usually changed into our pajamas in the living room, stood over that furnace register until we were all toasty warm and then darted for our beds. If it was bitter cold, Mama would put a hot water bottle wrapped in a flannel cloth in our bed to warm it up.

At an early age I remember we had an outhouse; but when I was seven we got a bathroom. Besides converting a pantry/closet next to the kitchen for the bathroom, the water supply system was changed. Instead of the open water tank in the attic, they installed a large cylindrical metal tank in the cellar. Now the pump out at the well not only had to supply the water but had to do so at a pressure to drive water from the cellar up to the bath and the kitchen. We felt very luxurious. In fact none our farm neighbors had indoor plumbing. The hot water still came from a tank which was a part of the kitchen wood stove.

Heat in the bathroom was from a kerosene heater. A hot bath in the winter was quite an operation. Hot water had to be brought from the kitchen after the kerosene heater had warmed the bathroom. You can be sure baths were done pretty quickly and not too often. A full bath was usually a once a week affair on Saturday night in the winter. Summer was different, but Mama was always insistent about us being clean all the time so kitchen wash-ups were frequent. When I was a little fellow, Mama used give me a bath in a big copper washtub right there in the kitchen where it was nice and warm. Then I put on my pajamas and raced for the bed which I hoped it had been warmed by a hot water bottle.

On the back of the house just outside the kitchen was a room with a flat roof—obviously an add on. It was not finished inside, but it was a place for the hand operated washing machine, storage of wood for the kitchen stove and pantry space for food. Of course, in winter or bad weather it served as a place to take off muddy boots or wet coats.

Above the kitchen was a small gable "room" with a child-size door that opened onto that flat roof. It was tight for an adult but big enough for a child to enter. Entry was by a ladder to the flat roof and then through the small door. Inside was a small space with enough head room for a child to stand up. In the center of the floor was a grate directly over the kitchen below. It was a sort of secret place for us children. It became our clubhouse. In winter we got heat from the cook stove in the kitchen below. And we could listen to all the adult conversation below as Mama and some my sisters prepared meals. Of course, in summer it was unbearably hot, but we seldom played up there; we were outside in the yard.

*Hilldene farmhouse viewed from the north. With all the shade
trees and grass yard, our farmhouse was the nicest of any around.*

Outside alongside the kitchen there were two separate small
buildings about ten feet from the main house. One was the smoke
house where we smoked our hams and bacon. The other was the spring
house where we kept milk, butter, eggs and anything else that needed
cooling. It had a concrete floor with a two foot wide channel around
two sides. Cold spring water ran through this channel and out a drain.
Containers of whatever needed to be cooled were simply set in the one
inch of cool water running in the channel. The spring house with its
concrete floor was cool enough for other things such as vegetables
and fruits. It was a great place to cool watermelons. I can remember
going in there in summer barefooted and feeling that delicious cool
damp air and cool floor. Only when we planned to make home made
ice cream did we have the luxury of ice. Of course, we had to buy ice
at Campbell's store in Doswell and that was quite a trip. So we didn't
have ice tea; we had cool tea.

Unlike many farm houses, ours had a nice fenced in yard with grass
and some trees. Just about forty feet outside the kitchen door was a large
honey locust tree. It was not a particularly pretty tree but we loved it
because in the fall it produced foot-long brown pods that contained a

sweet honey-like pulp inside. We chewed on the pods and spit out the seeds. Anything sweet was always popular with us kids.

Mama and Daddy had planted four black walnut trees when they bought the farm and by the time I could remember they were big and tall. They furnished much needed shade in summer and lots of walnuts in the fall. Other trees had been planted over the years so the yard had plenty of shade. We had a rope swing from a limb on one of those walnut trees. Many hours I spent in that swing fantasizing about traveling to far away places and meeting strange and wonderful people. On really hot summer days I can remember stretching out on my back in that cool grass under one of those big trees and staring up at the sky and the clouds passing over. One of my early summer chores was cutting the grass. We had a regular push lawn mower. My reward was a cool glass of lemonade or sweet milk when I was finished. I didn't get paid an allowance. There wasn't money for that. Besides, everyone had certain work expected of them and there was no complaining—well, maybe a little.

Our farmhouse was two miles from the little town of Doswell down a winding dirt road through woods. When you came out of the woods you could look across fields and see our farmhouse about one-quarter mile away. Our house had white siding with dark green shutters and trim. The roof was metal and painted the same shade of green. I thought our house was the prettiest one around. In fact, it was. Just beyond our fenced in yard, the land sloped down to the "flats," as we called that land. So our house was on a hill and the "flats" were like a valley. Maybe that's why my folks named our farm "Hilldene" which means "hill" and "valley." Of course, they may have also been influenced by a famous estate built in Manchester, Vermont, around the time they were married. It was the summer home of Robert Todd Lincoln, eldest son of President Lincoln. That famous estate was also named "Hildene," spelled differently from our farm's name. Anyway, the name of Hilldene stuck and the farm is known by that name to this day.

When Mama and Daddy bought the farm, it had several farm buildings and sheds but no barn. They soon decided that they needed a barn for the storage of hay, grain, farm machinery and the horses, cows and sheep. Hogs always had their separate hog pen separated from the barn. The story of the barn construction was told to me by my cousin, Latimer Watkins, aged 94.

"*Uncle Ira (my Daddy) decided that he could cut that stand of virgin pine trees on the south part of the farm and that would provide the necessary lumber. Still, there would be considerable expense and money was extremely short. So Uncle Ira wrote to his father, Grandfather Day in Maryland, and asked if he could borrow some money to help with the construction. Rough sketches and dimensions were included in the letter to give Grandfather Day an idea of the barn layout. The location of the barn was not yet decided. Now, Grandfather Day was familiar with the layout of Hilldene farm and the terrain. He remembered the slope down from the level of the farmhouse toward the flats. He figured that would be an ideal place to build a "bank barn," the favorite type built in his part of Maryland. A bank barn is built into the side of a hill so that the second level coincides with the upper level of the land. That way a team of horses can drive directly into the second level with its load of hay or grain making the unloading easy. The first level accommodates the livestock. Because the bank barn is built partially into the hill, the foundation and most of the first story is built of stone. Building stone was plentiful on the farms around the Maryland area where Grandfather Day lived. Grandfather Day agreed to loan some money to Uncle Ira and wrote describing his ideas of the type of barn that would be best. Much later after the barn had been built, Grandfather Day learned to his dismay that no bank barn had been built. Rather, the barn was built as a regular two-story wooden structure on the same level as the farmhouse about one hundred yards distant. The Hilldene farm was different from the Maryland farm; there was no suitable building stone. Grandfather Day had overlooked this important difference. Furthermore, when Uncle Ira had discussed the location of the barn with Aunt Sallie (Mama), she had been firm that no barn was to be built on that slope just below the house because it would be too close to the house. She was concerned about flies, the stench from the barn and the noise of the farm animals.*"

We had a large garden just outside our yard where we grew most of our summer vegetables. This was augmented by large plantings of sweet corn, potatoes, watermelons, cantaloupes and strawberries in one of our fields. We had a variety of fruit trees: apple, pear, cherry, plum and persimmon. It all took work, but we had a variety of good food to eat.

5

School

I was the youngest of the eight children in our family of four boys and four girls. Most of my brothers and sisters attended the same school, the Doswell Elementary School. In fact some of the same teachers taught my older brothers and sisters as taught me. Teacher turnover in the '30's was very low; jobs were scarce. Besides I think the teachers were very dedicated. And they were respected by the parents. In those days of the Depression, people held on to their jobs for survival. The school was a one story brick building with one classroom for each of the seven grades. It was located at the junction of the Chesapeake and Ohio Railroad and US Highway #l, just on the outskirts of the little town of Doswell. Most of the children who attended, walked to school although there were a couple school buses for those living farther out in the county.

I started school in the second grade at age seven. Mama had held me at home because of the two mile walk and because I had been sick. Among other sicknesses, I had whooping cough and pneumonia. Mama nursed me through the whooping cough but the pneumonia was bad enough that she had to call the doctor. Only in very extreme situations did we have the doctor; there was only one. In order to call for the doctor, someone had to ride a horse or drive the wagon the two miles to Doswell to make a telephone call for Dr. Wright. It might be half a day before he arrived. Calls for Dr. Wright were few. Mama had her own array of home remedies. There was castor oil for most anything. Iodine was put on all open cuts or abrasions. The pain from the iodine was excruciating but it certainly sterilized the wound! The one treatment I hated the most was Musterole. It was rubbed on your chest whenever you had a cough or chest congestion. Musterole was fiery hot and the fumes would burn your nostrils. However, it was effective.

Mama was very concerned that all her children get a good education. She was well educated herself and did a lot of reading to keep informed. The fact that she had been a teacher made it natural for her. She taught me the basics, letters and beginning to read, so I was not behind when I started school in second grade. My teacher in second grade was Miss Pollard, a matronly lady who was very good with children. Miss Pollard had taught four of my older brothers and sisters so she knew a lot about "those Day children".

Walking to school was not difficult for me except in really bad weather. It just took time. Our farm was two miles from Doswell. There was only one house, the Mitchell's, about one third of the way in from Doswell. My brother, Emil, walked with me until I began the fourth grade. After that he went earlier and came home later because he had to catch a school bus in Doswell for the seven mile ride to the Ashland High School. I remember the year he finished the seventh grade at Doswell. That year, 1935, they had an interesting program on graduation night. Emil was one of eleven to graduate from the seventh grade. I was in the third grade. As reported in the local newspaper, grades one to six put on a program called "A Spring Fantasy." Different members of the classes represented: Spring, Summer, Sweet South Wind, Cold North Wind, Jack Frost, Sun, The Boy, Will-O-Wisp and Bumblebees. In addition there were: Flowers and Butterflies. My part was the Sun. I remember my costume was basically a large round orange paper sun pinned to my shirt. I could just see over the top of it. I guess my red hair added to the effect. This was my earliest and only try to break into the world of drama. I don't think the production was intended to be a comedy but there sure was a lot of laughter in the audience that night!

When I was in the fifth grade, Emil left Ashland High to go to

Richmond to continue with his high school studies. He had gotten into some mischief at school and Mama and Daddy thought it best for him to change schools. In Richmond he lived with my older sister, Clara, while he was going to Thomas Jefferson High School. From then on I walked alone to school. I used to fantasize stories to entertain myself while I walked alone. I could continue the story the next day and remember all the characters that I had made up at the beginning. It was a way of passing the time while I walked. Sometimes I would meet up with the Mitchell boy, about my age, and we walked together to his house coming home or from his house on to school in the morning. In really severe snowy winter days, Daddy hitched up the two horses and took me in the old farm wagon. I remember how the snow would freeze to the iron wagon wheel rims when we broke through the ice as we crossed some of the streams and low places in the road. The snow would cling to the wheel rims in great clumps which made a jarring ride. By the time I was nine or ten, I walked myself regardless of the weather.

The school didn't have a cafeteria but it did have a little kitchen where they made soup during the winter months. All the children were expected to bring their own lunch; the soup was a little extra. On those cold winter days, I can still remember the aroma of vegetable soup that you could smell even in the classroom. It was served to all the kids in the lower grades. I guess they thought we hadn't had a good breakfast at home. Probably some of the kids hadn't. I know I always got a good breakfast at home. My breakfast was probably oatmeal, or eggs, sausage and cornbread—most likely left over and toasted in that big black cast iron cook stove in our kitchen. Anyway, I got soup along with the others to add to my lunch. It was so good!

My best friend in school was Lewis Carter. He lived in the town of Doswell close to the C & O tracks. His dad was a section man on the railroad and together with a crew of three or four was responsible for maintenance of a certain section of the railroad. They used one of those little four wheel cars that rode on the rail tracks and was propelled by two men pumping a lever, one man on each end. Lewis and his brother, Floyd, often walked the remaining one half mile with me to the school. Lewis was good in school. Floyd got "social promotions." He was not as smart as Lewis, but the teachers didn't know what to do with him so they just moved him up a grade each year. The other boy I sometimes joined up with was Grayson Taylor. He lived about a mile east of Doswell along the C & O railroad. One of the smartest children in my class was Mary Stuart Mason. Her father was the Rector of Fork Episcopal Church a few miles south of Doswell on the Old Gum Tree Road. He also came to preach at St. Martin's Episcopal Church in Doswell once a month. Also in my class was George Brown Oliver, the son of the banker in Doswell. We often competed for top grades in spelling and arithmetic.

I liked school. The teacher I most remember and respected and the one who taught me English grammar was Miss Tony. She was both the principal and the seventh grade teacher. She was a slight woman with black hair pulled back into a bun at the base of her neck. She had a slight tremor in her hands but when she wrote on the blackboard it was clear and firm. Stern but fair, she made the rules of grammar absolute laws. If you were going to list a series of items, they must always be preceded by a colon, never just a comma. Or when you introduced a thought beginning with "If" or "Because," that clause must always have a comma before you began the subject and predicate of the sentence that followed. She was so firm in emphasizing the do's and don'ts that I remember them clearly to this day. I learned more English grammar in that seventh grade than in all of my years of high school and college. And it stuck. Spelling was taught in all the grades leading up to the seventh, but that didn't mean that Miss Tony didn't emphasize it also in her class. A misspelled word in her class was a serious thing which could not be passed over lightly. We were sent to the big dictionary on the stand in the corner of the room to look it up and write the correct spelling on the blackboard. Embarrassing, you bet! But you were expected to take your writing seriously. If you didn't know the correct spelling, then you should look it up in the dictionary before you sent in your paper. Mama used a similar practice at home and we always had easy access to the dictionary. It was good discipline.

Homework was done on that big round oak table in the kitchen where it was warm from the wood cook stove. If I had difficulty with some of my homework, Mama was always available to help. Often while I was practicing spelling or solving arithmetic problems, she would busy herself with some kitchen duty in order to be near. Besides the assigned school work, she would often suggest something I should read in a newspaper or magazine. In addition to being nice and warm in the kitchen, we also had the best light there, our Coleman oil lamp with the mantle. It shone a good white light and was the best light in the house. When my homework was finished, Mama carried this lamp into the living room for reading or sewing. Our other lamps were the common kerosene wick type that gave a yellowish glow. They were really not very good although Daddy was usually reading the newspaper or a farm magazine by this light. Reading was very important to Mama and she encouraged me to do the same. We had books at home and I checked out others from our small library at school. I liked stories of adventure and history. To this day, I can't imagine anyone who does not enjoy reading.

The author at ten years old. Plenty of freckles and red hair.

Each year as we started a new grade there was the anticipation of new school books. By "new," I mean new to me. Of course new books were available but it was pretty customary to recycle the books— resell them to the grade below you. We always bought our books that way because it saved money. If you happened to have a brother or sister in the grade ahead of you then you would automatically get their books. I didn't have that situation. Emil, the next sibling to me, was four years older than I was, so I had to buy my books. It was obvious the books had been well used. The covers were pretty well worn and had marks throughout the pages. Many of the pencil marks could be erased, if you were careful not to tear the pages. We solved the cover problem by putting on new covers. The covers were furnished by the school. I believe the book manufacturers sent them along with the supply of new books each year. The covers were made of slick brown paper already cut to the right shape and size. They only needed to be fitted and glued. The night of the first day of school was the time to look over the books. Some of the worst marks needed to be erased and then a general look-see to get an idea of what lay ahead in that particular course. Next, it was time to get out the mucilage to fit and glue the slick brown covers on the books. There was a place to write the title of the book on the cover: Geography, Arithmetic, Spelling, or what have you. And, of course, a place for your name. That done, you had the books for the coming year. With the new covers I was always so proud of my books and anxious to learn all the things inside. I put them in my book bag, along with three or four pencils and some paper, and I was ready for school the next day.

Penmanship was an important subject and considerable time was spent on it. We used the Palmer method. We learned to write script; no printing was allowed. The strokes were meant to be graceful and to flow from one letter into the next. Exercises involved making continuous ovals that I always thought looked like long springs. We practiced on paper that had guide lines for the capital letters and lower case letters. You had to keep between the lines and make each letter carefully. We received a grade on penmanship just as we did on arithmetic and other subjects. My handwriting was never particularly good, but legible. Good handwriting was essential. Although typewriters were used in business, few families had them. Certainly a farm family struggling to make ends meet would be the last one to own a typewriter.

Recess time at school was an opportunity to play marbles which was one of my favorite games with the other boys. Every schoolboy under the age of about twelve had a collection of glass marbles. The cheaper ones were of varied colors, usually marbled; the prized ones were typically of one color, say blue or yellow, with the color uniform throughout the marble. These prized ones were called "Alleys" or "Aggies." Often the Alleys were slightly larger than the common marble and were used as "shooters." The shooters were called "Taws" by some but we never used that term. There are perhaps a dozen games of marbles, but we only played one which was played outside in the bare dirt. Any number of players could participate. First, an inner circle of about one foot diameter was drawn in the dirt. Then a larger circle of about five or six feet diameter was drawn about the inner circle. Each player placed an equal number of his cheap marbles in the inner ring. The first player placed his knuckle on the line of the outer ring and fired away with his shooter, attempting to knock one or more marbles out of the inner ring. If he did so, he pocketed that marble or marbles providing his shooter stayed in the larger ring. If so, he continued shooting as long as he could knock marbles out of the inner ring and his shooter stopped within the larger circle. When he failed, the next player tried his skill and luck. This continued until all marbles had been knocked out of the inner ring. The winner was the one who had captured the most marbles. Of course, there was much selling and trading of marbles among the boys. I typically kept a supply of marbles in a glass jar in my bedroom. If you ran out and couldn't buy any from the other boys, then Campbell's General Store in Doswell was a source. They came packaged about a dozen in a little red mesh bag. There were other marble games that could be played indoors on a carpet. But those never figured into my play; we didn't have a carpet big enough for those games.

If you played marbles, there were two telltale signs: dirty knuckles on the right hand and dirty knees on your pants. So when we played at recess at school we tried to brush off the dirt from our pants and to race by the wash-up sink before we returned to class. If I was at home, the clean up was easier but Mama always knew what I had been doing.

Just about every boy in grammar school had a pocket knife, so it was natural for us to also play games involving our pocket knives. If I was lucky and careful, I would have my knife all year that had come with my Sears Roebuck lace-up boots. If I got a new pair of boots this season, I would also get a new knife. At school, one game we played with our pocket knives was called Mumbly Peg. It could be played by any number of players, but usually only involved two or three. Players took turns tossing the knife from various positions so that the blade stuck in the ground each time. A number of different positions, sometimes called stunts, were used in sequence until the player failed to throw his knife and have it stick upright in the ground. When that happened, the action passed to the next player. The winner was the first one to perform successfully all the required stunts in sequence; the loser was the last one to complete all the stunts. Before we began the game, we decided on the stunts and their sequence. Here are a few typical stunts we used:

- The knife was placed on the right hand, palm up, with the blade toward the finger tips. The toss was made by rotating the hand up and over with palm down thus sending the knife into the ground.
- With the right hand closed, the knife was placed across the fingernails with the blade toward the right. The tosser rotated his hand sending the knife toward the ground.
- With the fingers spread on the right hand, palm down, the knife was laid across the knuckles, blade pointing to the right. The tosser must rotate his hand to the left causing the knife to rotate and stick in the ground.
- The knife was held by the blade and thrown so it rotated before it stuck in the ground.
- Similar to the preceding except the throw was made behind the back.

All of the previous are repeated except the throw was done with the left hand.

These are only a few of the ingenious stunts that the players thought up to make the game more challenging. The winner then drove a short wooden peg as far into the ground as he could with three blows of his knife handle plus three additional blows with his eyes closed. If he was clever, the peg would be completely driven into the ground. The loser of the game then had to remove the peg with his teeth. The result was usually a dirt-smeared face for the loser amid howls of laughter from the other players. This was the origin of the name Mumbly Peg.

The first of May, May Day, was a big event at school. The main thing we had were relay races against other schools. For this competition we rode a school bus to Ashland, seven miles, where children from all over Hanover County were gathered. Of course, we had practiced for several weeks before we came to the countywide competition. With my long legs, I was a pretty good runner. I was tall for my age and definitely on the skinny side. Many times I was taunted by some of the older boys, "Say, Red, you must eat a lot of string beans. You sure are skinny!"

That was invariably followed by a burst of laughter. My red hair and freckles often prompted similar comments. At first such comments hurt, but little by little I got used to them.

Mama always told me, "LeRoy, don't let those silly boys bother you. Red hair is a mark of distinction. Did you know George Washington had red hair? Of course, he wore a white wig most of the time so most people don't know that. Lots of famous people have red hair."

Several of my sisters had red hair of various shades. And, of course, Mama had dark auburn hair. However, I was the only boy in our family with red hair. It wasn't that common in our school, either.

I loved the competition of the May Day relay races. Boys and girls competed separately. We had a paper number pinned on the back of our shirt which made us feel like real athletes. It was usually warm enough by May first that we could even run barefooted. Of course, some of the kids had tennis shoes. Sometimes I had them but most times I just ran barefooted which I thought was faster. Usually the relay races had four teams competing in each race. Each team consisted of three boys.

We ran one third of the way around the track and passed our baton to the next member of our team. It was necessary to pass the baton before we reached a line and not to drop it in the process. The baton was a ten-inch length of broom stick that we had made at school. If our team won in the first race, we got to race again against teams from other schools. This continued until the "grand winner" was determined. It was great fun to run with my classmates and even better when we won.

After the races, we sat in groups on the grass and ate our lunches. I always carried my lunch in a black lunch box that held a thermos bottle. Usually I had milk in the thermos although sometimes Mama would make hot tea. When all the races were over and the winning teams received their ribbons, we boarded the bus for the return trip to Doswell. What an exciting day! There was the added pleasure that there were only a few more weeks and school would be out for the summer! Good times were coming!

6

Playtime

I made many of my own toys. Early on when I was quite young, I used to amuse myself by rolling a hoop with a wire pusher. The hoop was most likely a rim off the wheel of a baby carriage or some piece of farm equipment or maybe a play wagon. It couldn't be too small or it was impossible to control. Remember, we were playing in the dirt road running beside the barn. No paved surface for us. You guided the hoop and pushed it at the same time with a piece of heavy wire bent in the shape of a U and with a handle of comfortable length. The hoop was started rolling with a gentle push and then continued by putting the U on the rim and guiding and pushing at the same time. With a little practice you could maneuver it any way you chose. It was a simple toy for playing by yourself. Of course, a larger version of the same game was to roll a tire or large wheel just by pushing and guiding it with your hand.

When I was about seven years old I became very interested in deep sea divers and submarines. I read some books on them and decided to make some toys that I could use. The diver was simple. I carved the shape of a man out of pine wood, crude but recognizable. The figure was about six inches tall. Then I cut an old inner tube in a shape to approximate the body of the wooden man. One piece for the front and one for the back. With needle and thread, I sewed the front and back together encasing the wooden man. I used a small pill bottle for the helmet. I loaded the diver with small weights, pieces of lead and nails, until he was just nearly neutrally buoyant—just able to sink at a slow rate while maintaining an upright position. At that time we had a large open circular water tank near the barn for the animals to use. It was a great place to play with my diver and also the submarine.

Now the submarine I made was a little more involved. Again, I carved the sub from a block of pine. I remember it well. The submarine was about ten inches long. I used a finishing nail, bent just below the head of the nail, as the periscope. I drove small brads (nails) around the perimeter of the forward deck and connected them with light wire to simulate the railing on the foredeck. On the bottom of the sub I fastened two pieces of metal extending down about an inch at the bow and stern of the sub. Between these two pieces I stretched a rubber band and fastened a propeller at the stern. I had built rubber powered model airplanes and I knew how to fashion a rubber powered drive system for the sub. I weighted the sub with lead until the deck was just awash. So far, so good. I put on diving planes toward the front of the sub, made with sheet metal, and bent them up to force the bow down when the sub was driven through the water by the rubber band power system. Once the rubber band had unwound and furnished no more power to the prop, the sub would slow and gradually come to the surface. Perfect. A controlled dive. I spent many hours playing with that sub in the circular watering tank at the barn. I was so pleased with its ability to dive and then return to the surface that I thought it would be fun to try it at the swimming hole at the river. Unfortunately, I hadn't realized that the current would affect it so much. The sub did its usual dive but never surfaced again. It was swept down stream and I lost my prized toy.

I loved baseball. We played baseball during recess at school and sometimes I would go out to Doswell and play with the Carter boys, Lewis and Floyd. But most of the time, I was alone and I invented a game to practice baseball by myself. There was a good grassy plot along the side of the barn. I could throw a rubber ball against the side of the barn and catch it on the rebound. The barn had regular siding on it with one board overlapping the next. Depending where the ball hit the siding, on the flat surface or on an edge, the return would be a high fly or a straight ball or, even a grounder, if I threw it low. I could get a lot of practice fielding various balls just by throwing it against the barn. Of course, this did nothing for my batting, which wasn't overly good. Anyway, I could imagine a ball game with me playing center field and get a lot of practice catching flies even though I was alone. I had to make up a lot of games like this which involved imagination mixed with action that I could do by myself.

When I was in the fifth grade I wanted a bicycle in the worst way. Sure enough I got one for Christmas. It was blue with white pin stripes. Oh, what a sense of freedom that bike gave me! Now I could ride out to Doswell in fifteen or twenty minutes instead of walking it in forty five minutes. In the long summer evenings after we had our supper, I sometimes rode out to Doswell to play with the Carter boys, usually some baseball. I had a basket on the handlebars where I carried my baseball glove or whatever. I got a siren from Sears and Roebuck for my bike. The spindle drive for the siren could be pressed against the side of the tire by a chain pull on the handlebars. Somehow that siren made me feel more important. Sirens on bikes were popular in those days. Another amusement was to fasten a piece of cardboard to the fork of the front wheel and let it extend in to touch the spokes. When the wheel rotated, the cardboard made a "put-put" sound which increased in frequency as you speeded up the bike. With a little imagination it sounded like a motor on your bike. My bicycle made me feel I could go anywhere; actually, I seldom rode it farther than the town of Doswell but there was that great feeling of independence and freedom. Sometimes in the summer I would ride it to Doswell all the way through town to the highway and up to the gas station on the main highway. They had a big red box just outside of the door with "Coca Cola" painted on it. Inside were all sorts of bottled drinks: Orange Crush, Doctor Pepper, RC Cola, Pepsi Cola, Root Beer and, of course, Coca Cola. Chunks of ice floated between the bottles keeping everything ice cold. I would select one of those delicious cold drinks, maybe a RC Cola, and give the man a nickel. The drink tasted so good because it was ice cold, a treat for me. I would sit down on the pavement in the shade and lean back against the gas pump; then I could watch all the highway traffic go by while I enjoyed my drink. Such luxury.

My playmates visiting from the city, nieces, Gretchen (kneeling), Evelyn (with kittens) and nephew, Roger, with his trusty rubber band gun. I am in the center.

The game of "Cowboys and Indians" or "Cops and Robbers" or any variation that involved combat was a favorite. We had two versions: cap pistols or rubber band guns. Most boys our age had a couple of cap pistols. A roll of caps was put into the pistol with the end under the hammer. Each time the hammer fired a cap, the roll advanced to the next cap. Playing with these cap pistols involved a lot of imagination. Of course, there was a lot of contention between the combatants arguing whether or not they had been shot. The other version of the game used rubber band guns. We made our own rubber band guns. The rubber bands were sections cut out of old inner tubes, about one half inch wide. Tires and inner tubes failed pretty often in those days so there were usually discarded inner tubes that couldn't be patched at the filling station on US #1 highway just outside of Doswell. I used to ride my bicycle out there and ask if I could have one or two. One pretty good inner tube would last for a long time as our source of "ammunition" for our play. There were several types of rubber band guns. First, the gun could be in the form of a pistol which we sawed out of a piece of pine board. It was usually just an L-shaped gun with the long part being the barrel. We fastened two wooden clothes pins to the back of the handle or stock. Two rubber bands were stretched over the barrel and back to the stock where they were each held by a clothes pin. You fired the rubber band by pressing the clothes pin with your thumb. That gave you two shots. The effective range was not more than about ten, maybe fifteen feet. An improved design was good for four shots. This model was similar in shape but instead of the clothes pins we carved four notches in the back of the stock. Each rubber band was stretched over the tip of the "barrel" and secured in one of the notches beginning with the top notch. That meant the first shot was made when you rolled the rubber band out of the bottom notch and off the stock with your thumb. With a little practice you could get off four shots in a manner of seconds. We learned to increase the range by just lengthening the barrel thereby stretching the band more. Roger, my nephew, made a version like a double barrel rifle. Using the four-notch scheme, he could have eight shots with a much longer range. So as not to be outgunned, we soon all built one of the long range double barrel versions. The shots were harmless and didn't even sting unless you fired at a very close range. The trick was not to lose all your "ammunition" to the other team. After a battle we always had to hunt for the errant shots and even then sit down and cut out some more bands from an inner tube. These battles with different imaginary characters could keep us occupied for hours.

A lot of our play was influenced by things we read. There were books called "Big Little Books." These books were about four by four inches and maybe two inches thick. They were versions of comic books. These "Big Little Books" contained stories about many of the characters in the funny pages: Dick Tracy, Tarzan, Popeye and others. Usually one of my older brothers or sisters would bring up the Sunday edition of the Richmond News Leader when they came on the weekend. That was a chance to read all the comics or funny pages as we called them. There were the adventures of Flash Gordon, Superman, Little Orphan Annie and Li'l Abner. I was particularly interested in Tarzan. I had seen one of the Tarzan movies and thought how exciting it would be to swing from tree to tree and swim in that crystal clear water. Gretchen, Roger and I did try to imitate Tarzan in our woods. We found grape vines that grew up some of the trees, cut them at the base and swung on them. The problem was we often collided with the tree when we tried to get a really good swing. Oh, but we had fun anyway!

Cowboys always fascinated me. Living on a farm and loving the outdoors, I could identify with them. Cowboy movies and books about the Wild West were very popular. This was the time of the movie cowboys: Tom Mix, Hopalong Cassidy, Gene Autry and others. I wanted to learn to twirl a lasso like I saw them do in the movies. I finally learned that the trick to success was to have a stiff rope and a knot that didn't slip too easily. That way I could maintain a circle with the lasso. Of course, all the rope I could find around the barn was usually too limp but at least I could make the knot so it wouldn't slip. I practiced lassoing fence posts, tree stumps and anything that didn't move. One day I decided that I was getting good enough at lassoing to give it a try on something that moved. Why not the calf that was out in the pasture? That would be just like the cowboys; I could pretend I was on a horse. I slipped through the gate and moved along the fence keeping the mother cow between me and the calf. Suddenly the calf spied me and took off across the pasture. I ran after him with the lasso at the ready. The first throw missed and he ran ahead twenty paces and then stopped and looked back at me. I readied my lasso and walked slowly toward him but he took off running before I got within lasso range. We both raced across the pasture and I gave a throw when I was close behind him. The lasso sailed over his head and dropped around his neck. I was so surprised that I had lassoed him! I stopped running but he continued and when he reached the end of the rope he jerked me off my feet. I was suddenly being dragged on my stomach across the pasture. I was so surprised I forgot to let go of the rope. That calf was so much stronger than I expected! In a few seconds I did let go of the rope after he had dragged me some distance. I learned that lassoing wasn't as easy as it looked in the movies.

The adults seldom played with the children. Nor did they supervise us unless it was necessary to settle an argument or break up an occasional fight. One game we did play with the adults, usually one of my older brothers, was horseshoes. Being on the farm, we always had a supply of old horseshoes. We had a permanent setup in one corner of our yard. Two strong metal stakes were driven in the ground about forty feet apart. A dirt area of about four feet by four feet surrounded each stake. Sand or soft earth in that box area was good to keep the horseshoes from bouncing too much. Often two adults would play with two of us children. We would pair off with one adult and one child at each end. If there were only two people playing, we would each throw our two horseshoes in turn and then walk to the stake, determine our score depending on the position of the horseshoes and then throw at the other stake. The winner was the first player to achieve forty points. This is the way we kept score:

- One point for the closest horseshoe to the stake. However, to qualify the shoe must be within a distance equal or less than the measurement across the open end of the horseshoe. This was handy as a horseshoe could be used for the measurement.
- A leaner against the stake was worth three points.
- A ringer around the stake was worth five points.
- Points were determined after both players had thrown. Part of the strategy was to knock your opponent's shoes out of position and deny him points.

There were basically two pitching styles. One method was to sail the horseshoe so it rotated, but remained parallel to the ground along its trajectory toward the stake. The other style was to impart a flipping motion to the horseshoe so that it tumbled end over end as it flew toward the stake. A really good pitch using this second technique would have the shoe land flat with the open end toward the stake about a foot in front of the stake. The shoe would then slide right into a perfect position as a "ringer." In this case, it was almost impossible for your opponent to knock your horseshoe out of position and deny you the points for a ringer. If you were careful and not wipe your hands on your pants, this was a game you could play even after you had on your good Sunday clothes. Not so with a game like marbles.

There were times when one of my older sisters or Mama would play with us. That was when we played a board game like Monopoly. Monopoly could keep us occupied for hours on a cold rainy afternoon or night. Each player started with an equal amount of play money. A player advanced around the board according to his throw of the dice. A stop on the board gave him the opportunity to buy a particular piece of real estate or perhaps a railroad. If he had enough money he could also buy a hotel and place it on his real estate. Then, if another player landed on his real estate, he would have to pay rent to the owner. Several strategies could be used which made the game interesting. Players could number from two to four or six. The game of Monopoly came out in 1935 and quickly became popular. Even today it is one of the most popular board games played around the world.

We also played another game called Carom. It was played on a large wooden board that had pockets at the corners similar to a pool table. Instead of balls, wooden discs or wooden rings, called strikers, were flicked with the index finger to knock other discs into the pockets. The object of the game was to knock as many as possible of your color discs into the pockets. If you failed to knock all of them in, your opponent then had his chance to play. The first player who got all of his color discs in the pockets was declared the winner.

Of course, we also played card games and checkers. We could always find things to entertain us even when we were stuck in the house.

7

Winter

Life on the farm was very much regulated by the seasons of the year. The pace on the farm slowed in winter, but there was still much that had to be done. Food, heat and care of the animals were the essentials. This was also school time for the children. In addition, this was the time for repair of farm and household items. Fences had to be inspected and repaired. The dirt road to Doswell always needed repair, especially in the winter and early spring when the heavy rains came. The perpetual "chores" were always there. But there was time for winter play: skating on ice ponds in the fields or sledding down the hill by the barn when we had snow.

Daddy was always the one to milk the one or two Holstein cows we had. I don't remember any of my brothers ever having this job. Daddy showed me a couple times how to grasp the teats of the cow's bag and pull down to get a stream of milk but he never asked me to do the milking. Somehow, I think he might have felt that was his job and maybe even enjoyed it. There were other jobs he expected me to do. Often, Daddy asked me to throw down hay from the barn loft for the horse and mule and the cows. Next I brought in buckets of ears of corn from the corn crib for all of the animals. Each stall had a water bucket that needed filling after the ice was knocked out. When the barn chores were done, I had to tend the two chicken houses. The water pans were outside and usually frozen, but a bucket of hot water from the kitchen solved that problem. Then I gave them some grain, a mixture of corn and wheat. We had a machine, hand cranked, that shelled the corn from the ears. We always kept a supply of shelled corn on hand. The chickens got shelled corn; the animals could eat it on the cob.

Now it was time to hurry back to the house for a hot breakfast. That could be oatmeal and cornbread or maybe eggs and pork sausage with hominy. My favorite was buckwheat pancakes with some pork sausage. For a drink we always had milk available. Sometimes Mama would make hot cocoa; she and Daddy always had coffee. Hominy was made from whole grains of corn as opposed to grits which were ground corn. Both were cooked in boiling water and served hot as a side dish. We had hominy; I don't remember ever having grits. Grits was more common farther south than Virginia.

After breakfast I dressed quickly for school wearing those corduroy knickers, wool knee socks and my lace-up leather boots with the pocketknife on the side. If it was really cold, I'd wear either a knit stocking hat or my beloved Sears Roebuck "aviator's helmet" with goggles and chin strap. When I wore that helmet, I could imagine flying one of those biplanes I read about in "Air Trails" magazine. School began at nine so I needed to leave home by eight o'clock to walk the two miles. School was out at three o'clock. On the way home from the schoolhouse through the town of Doswell, I passed by Allen's Store and Post Office. I would stop to pick up our mail. If I didn't waste any time talking to Lewis Carter or Grayson Taylor, I could make it home by four o'clock. In the short days of winter, less than an hour of daylight remained for chores to be done before supper. Supper was our evening meal; dinner came in the middle of the day. After I changed into my work clothes, I went into the kitchen to see if there was anything I could grab to eat as I headed outdoors. Mama usually had some cornbread fritters which she called "scratch-backs" on the back of the stove. These were crispy, really hard, and had a delicious crust, particularly on the bottom and edges. They were made mostly of cornmeal, water, shortening, salt and a little sugar. Mama cooked them with a generous amount of fat in her favorite black iron frying pan. Here's her recipe:

Scratch-backs

1 cup of cornmeal	*2-3 tablespoon milk*
1 tablespoon sugar	*1-2 tablespoon lard*
½ teaspoon salt	*2-3 tablespoon butter*
1 cup boiling water	

Combine all the ingredients except the lard and the butter. The resulting batter should drop easily off a tablespoon. When the lard and butter is sizzling hot in the frying pan, drop in a tablespoon of the batter for each fritter. They will be thin with crisp edges and a crusty bottom in just a couple minutes. Delicious served hot or cold with butter, jam or honey.

One or two of these "scratch-backs" stuffed in my jacket pocket and I was all set to go to work. Evening chores were similar to morning ones except I needed to get in some wood for the kitchen cook stove, the fireplace and also the cellar furnace. Of course, when I made the rounds of the chicken houses, I picked up the eggs of the day.

I had a little wagon for bringing in the wood which worked if there was no snow on the ground. If we had snow, I had a wooden sled that I used to haul the firewood. I had to bring it about 100 yards from the woodpile near the barn to the house. That's where Daddy sawed up the wood with a circular saw belt-driven by a one-cylinder gas engine. I was never allowed to work that saw. It was a frightening thing with no guard and made an earsplitting high pitch whine when it was up to speed for sawing. I stacked the small firewood for the kitchen cook stove in that room just off the kitchen where it was dry and handy. Larger firewood, six to ten inches in diameter, was put down a chute to the cellar for the wood furnace. Then there was the fireplace wood in somewhat longer pieces which I stacked on the porch just outside our front door. Every few days I needed to split some kindling which was needed to start fires. Whenever we gathered dead trees from the woods, we were always on the lookout for the roots and knots of decayed pine trees. Those contained what was called "fat wood," which was rich in turpentine. Split into small pieces this "fat wood" made excellent kindling. I kept a box of it in the unfinished room just off the kitchen. Of course the kitchen wood stove was always going and also the furnace but we usually lit the living room fireplace after supper. To make it ready to light off, I laid the fire. First, I put in some of that kindling, then small wood and finally a couple of logs. The fireplace would warm you good if you stood up close to it. Even if it didn't provide much heat, it always gave the room a cheery atmosphere. It was good to stand in front of for a few minutes just before running off to those cold bedrooms. In addition to the firewood detail, sometimes if the weather was not too bad then the sheep were taken to pasture; they needed to be rounded up and gotten into the barn for the night.

Often, if Mama had been unusually busy that day, she would ask me to prepare the oil lamps for use that night. They had to be filled with kerosene and the wicks trimmed and the glass chimneys wiped or washed clear if they were smoked. This was a daily task that had to be done if we were to have light at night.

By the time I had finished these jobs, it was nearly dark and time for supper. Mama did a lot of canning: vegetables and fruits in summer and meat in the fall when we butchered a heifer and/or a hog. So supper was a substantial meal of canned meat and vegetables plus Irish or sweet potatoes from the cellar. Hot bread, either cornbread or biscuits, would top off the meal. Milk was always available for us kids and the adults had coffee or tea. We might have applesauce or canned peaches for desert, but they were usually reserved for weekends.

After supper was homework time for about an hour at that big round table in the kitchen, where it was nice and warm. For entertainment maybe we would play some records on our wind-up Victrola in the living room. We had a collection of records: Al Jolson and other singers of his time and some martial band music of Germany, France and the US. I liked that band music. There was always reading and time for talking about events of the day. Of course, like all farmers, Daddy was always interested in what the weather would be the next few days. Weather was all important and determined what activities could be done outside.

Daddy would always step outside and scan the skies before he went to bed and then make his prediction as to tomorrow's weather. There was no other source of information.

Both Emil and I (with helmet) built and flew rubber powered
model airplanes. My interest in airplanes continued my whole life.

Bedtime was around nine o'clock. It was hard to leave the warmth of the living room and go to those cold bedrooms. The warmest place was over that big circular register where the heat came directly from the furnace in the cellar. Of course, you could also get warm if you stayed close to the fireplace. Both of these were in the living room but it was all right to undress there before a quick good night and a dash for the bedroom. If it was particularly cold, Mama would fix a hot water bottle wrapped in flannel to warm the bed. Boy, that really felt good on your feet when you slipped into those cold sheets.

I remember a lot of snow and cold weather when I was growing up. We had a perfect hill for sledding near the barn. Emil and I had a lot of fun playing on that hill. Often on weekends, even in winter, Janice and Carl would drive up to the farm bringing their children, Evelyn,

Roger and Gretchen. Gretchen was a year younger than I, Roger a year older and Evelyn several years older. Roger and Gretchen were my playmates. We could find all kinds of outside things to do in winter including sledding if there was snow. If the snow was wet, we would pack down a run by walking up and down the hill, tramping with our boots. But the ideal condition, one we always wished for but seldom had, was for the snow to have a crust on it strong enough to support us on our Flexible Flyer sleds. Then we could literally fly down the hill going in any direction, over hummocks and across ditches, with a long coast on the flat road at the bottom. The only problem occurred if the crust was just barely strong enough to hold us. In a case like that, sometimes the sled runners would break through the crust if you hit a dip and the sled would stop suddenly throwing you off into the hard crusty snow. That would often result in a scraped face as you slid along the icy snow on your stomach. Oh, but it was worth it to have such speed and freedom to guide your sled anywhere you chose!

Of course, inside we played board games like Monopoly and entertained ourselves with whatever toys we had. Because my sister Janice was the oldest of the children and I was the youngest, her children were my same age and really like brothers and sisters. Janice was a generation away from me. In fact, she helped to deliver me before Dr. Wright made it to our house. But that's another story.

The fields on the west side of our house had several low places which collected rain forming shallow ponds. These froze easily and made good places to skate or play with our sleds. I liked to get a large piece of cardboard which acted as my sail and sit on my Flexible Flyer and have the wind whiz me across the ice. I imagined I was in an iceboat and racing across some lake in Wisconsin. I always wanted to sail in an iceboat, but this was as close as I ever got to it. Nevertheless, I had a lot of fun with my "cardboard-sled" iceboat.

Winter was a good time to build model airplanes. Emil and I built free flight models of balsa and tissue. I had a Wakefield about twenty four inches in wingspan that was a really good flyer. Of course, we had all the space in the world to fly them in the surrounding fields. Solid scale models were also one of my interests. One winter night I was building a solid model of the PBY Catalina flying boat on a building board in the living room. There was a lot of sanding of the balsa to get the fuselage to the rounded shape. It was a cold night and, as usual, we had a fire in the fireplace as well as one in the furnace in the cellar. I decided to stop working on the model for the night. I took the building board with its pile of balsa dust and gingerly dumped the dust into the fireplace. There was a muffled boom as all that balsa dust ignited.

Mama called out, "What did you do?"

"Nothing," was my lame answer.

Just then there was a low pitch roar and we knew that the chimney was on fire. Daddy and I raced outside and saw flames coming out of the chimney. That's when I became really scared. The balsa dust had ignited the creosote and tar in the walls of the chimney left there from burning too much pine wood. We had to get that fire out! Daddy got a couple buckets of water from the spring house, filled them, gave one to me and told me to climb the ladder to that roof just off the kitchen. From there I made my way up to the main roof and splashed the water into the fireplace chimney. In my hurry and fear of getting burned from the fire coming out of the chimney, the first bucket wasn't enough to douse the fire. I went back down the roof to where Daddy handed me another bucket and I repeated the process. After four buckets the fire was out and I came down to see the mess in the fireplace and to get a lecture on fire safety. I learned about "combustible materials" and how chimney fires can be started. Actually, since we contained the fire after a few minutes, it did a good thing by burning out the residue in the chimney. But next time we might not be so lucky. The danger was that the wood framing around the chimney could be ignited by a hot chimney and then there would be a house on fire. A house fire in an isolated farmhouse like ours spelled sure disaster. Well, I learned a lesson and never did dump balsa dust in the fireplace again. However, that didn't stop my airplane model building.

Sometimes on a cold winter night after Mama had cleaned up the kitchen from supper, she would suggest making some cookies. The wood cook stove was still warm and it could be brought up to baking temperature with a little "poking and some wood."

"LeRoy, how would you like to bake some cookies?" Mama inquired.

"That would be great. Could we bake sugar cookies?" I loved cookies. "But I thought you said yesterday that we were about out of sugar?"

"We are but we can substitute honey—we have plenty of that. You know, you have to make do with what you have. Get down my cooking book from that shelf and let's have a look. You find the recipe for sugar cookies while I get out some flour." Mama was a wonderful cook and I always enjoyed making things with her.

"You'd better poke up the stove a little and put in some more wood. It'll heat up while we mix the dough."

After I put wood in the stove, I opened Mama's cook book and found the recipe for the cookies. Mama knew the recipe by heart but she just wanted to teach me how to read it and mix the dough. She placed the flour bucket on the table and sat down in a chair beside me.

"You read the recipe and we'll get all the ingredients out here on the table before we start."

"We need two cups of flour," I began.

"Yes, why don't you read through the whole recipe before we start," Mama said.

"And, one and half teaspoons of baking powder, one half-teaspoon salt, one half cup of butter, one cup of sugar, one egg and one teaspoon of vanilla. That's all." I looked at her for further instructions.

"Alright. Now you go out to the pantry and bring in the butter and get a jar of that clear honey, no comb. I'll put the other things right here on the table and then you can start measuring and we'll mix the dough," Mama instructed.

"Now we're ready to begin," Mama said. "Use that measuring cup and that big spoon to measure out two cups of flour into the mixing bowl. Add your salt and baking powder. Mix it up good. "

"Now do I add the honey and the other stuff?" I inquired.

"No, we'll mix those other things in this small bowl and then add it to the flour. In place of the one cup of sugar we can use about three-quarters of a cup of honey because honey is sweeter. Put in your egg, the butter and vanilla with the honey and stir it good until it is thoroughly mixed." Mama was letting me do all the mixing while she observed.

When I had combined the liquid ingredients with the flour mix, the result was a little on the thin side. "Mama, this looks more like pancake mix that cookie dough. Did I do something wrong?"

"No, it's because we used honey instead of sugar. That gave us a bit more liquid. Just add a tablespoon of flour and mix it in. Keep adding a spoonful at a time until you get a stiff dough. Then we can roll it out and cut out the cookies." Mama always seemed to know what to do; it was all those years of cooking.

By the time we had rolled out the dough and cut out the cookies, the stove was hot and Mama put in a pan of the cookies to bake. A few minutes later she took them out and the room was filled with that delicious aroma of freshly baked sugar cookies.

"Would you like one while they're hot?" Mama said, smiling with a twinkle in her eye. "Take a couple into your Daddy. He's reading in the living room."

Nothing tasted better than those sugar cookies. They were even better because I had mixed them up myself—with a little help.

The two-mile dirt road from Doswell to our place always needed some repair. It did not have a crown but rather two ruts in most places which collected water and froze in the winter. Some sections were sandy and that was good; other stretches were a type of clay that turned to a sort of stiff mush when it was wet. One of the worst sections was the stretch of road that exited the woods and bordered the pasture on the way to our house. It was perhaps four hundred yards long. It bordered those flat fields that collected rain in winter and froze into the ice ponds that I used for my "cardboard ice boating" on my Flexible Flyer sled. When this stretch of road was frozen it was all right. Because it was in the open and not shaded by the woods, it was the first part of our road to thaw. That's when it turned into a quagmire. About the only auto traffic we had was when one of my older brothers or sisters came up from Richmond for a Sunday visit. Many times when they left, that stretch of road had thawed and they got stuck. Someone would come back to the house and call for Daddy to come with the horses and pull them out. So repair of this part of our road was the first priority in the winter. All we could do was haul sand with the farm wagon, fill in the ruts and try to improve the drainage. We got our sand from a sand pit on the edge of our property down toward the river. It was a job I did with Daddy many times; it had to be done at least once every winter. We would hitch up our mule, Molly, and our horse, Albert, to the farm wagon, get our shovels and head for the sandpit. The wagon was built so you could take off the sides, front and back. The floor of the wagon consisted of two by six boards. We drove the wagon down into the sandpit and shoveled in as much sand as the team could pull out of there. Then back to the section of the road to be repaired and stopped the wagon directly over the bad ruts. Instead of having to shovel the sand out of the wagon, Daddy had a clever scheme. He removed the front and rear ends of the wagon, leaving only the side boards in place. Then he got at the front and I was at the rear and we turned each of the floor planks on its side and dumped the sand. It was hard work but it was easier than shoveling the sand out of the wagon. All that remained after we had dumped the sand was to smooth it out. Each load of sand only repaired about ten feet along the road so it took many trips to the sandpit to improve that one section of road. It was a two-person operation that we usually did on Saturday because the other days I was in school.

The short dark days of winter slowly lengthened as we got closer to spring. Sometimes it seemed that spring would never come. But, of course, it always did and with it a change in the tempo of farm activities.

8

Spring

Spring was a glorious time on the farm. The whole world was awakening: with flowers and trees blooming, warming days and the birds returning. The very first bloom was always a crocus. Mama always had some planted in a flower bed outside the kitchen window that faced south. Sometimes if we had a late snow, the crocus would push up through the snow and show its yellow or purple bloom to signal that spring was not far off. Next would be the redbud trees with their tiny pinkish white bloom followed by the wild cherry trees. Our own fruit cherry trees bloomed with a profusion of white blossoms alongside the hill sloping down from our farmhouse. Jonquils, tucked away in flower beds around our yard, put up their long stems and soon displayed their white and yellow blossoms. Our apple trees made their show with a crown of white blooms on each tree. When the dogwood trees in the woods bloomed, they made splashes of white that looked like patches of snow from our farmhouse. Before long the trees and shrubs began to leaf out and show their green. Every way I looked outside there were increasing signs of the coming spring. Oh, how welcome it was after the long dark days of winter.

"Did you hear the flock of geese fly over just now?" I inquired as I came into the kitchen from feeding the chickens. "There must have been fifteen or twenty all flying in a vee formation. They were heading north. I wonder how far they will fly today."

"Yes, I heard them," Mama replied, as she took a pan of cornbread out of the oven for our breakfast. "They are headed for Canada so they have a long way to fly."

"Is that why they are called Canada geese? Why do they have to go up there?" I was always full of questions.

"Because that's where they make their nests and raise their babies. In the fall those young baby geese have to be strong enough to fly back down here with their parents. Isn't that something?" Mama said. "Now, wash up. Breakfast is ready. Call your daddy; he's shaving in the bathroom."

Spring was also the time when the baby lambs, calves and piglets were born. Baby chicks and young turkeys were hatched also. Caring for the baby chicks and the young turkeys was quite a chore. We had a large round metal chicken coop we called an "incubator." In the center it had a circular metal partition that left an open space about eighteen inches in diameter. We put a lighted kerosene lantern in that open center space to provide warmth for the chicks during those cool spring nights. Straw was spread on the floor of the incubator for the comfort of the chicks. Of course, the chicks all crowded toward that center partition and the warmth from the lantern. Often in the morning, we would find them piled on top of each other and several that had been killed in the process. We always lost some of the chicks but it was the best we had to keep a number of them warm while they were so young. Real disaster came if that kerosene lantern went out during the night. If that happened, probably most of the chicks would be dead in the morning. We needed those young chickens for food the coming year.

Spring was also a time for playing outside after a long dreary winter. For one thing, it was kite flying time. Sometimes I had a kite that I had bought at the store but often I made my own. We covered our homemade kites with brown paper or sometimes with tissue paper. The tail of the kite was an important part for stable flying. It was usually made of strips of old cloth knotted together. If the wind was strong, then a longer tail was necessary to keep the kite stable. By experimenting with the length of tail, I could make the kite very maneuverable. I loved watching my kite soar and making it dive and climb. Things that flew always fascinated me even if they were attached to a string. I could fantasize that my kite was a biplane fighting the enemy. Kite flying was a good solo play for me. Sometimes the wind was so cold I flew my kite with gloves on, but it was still fun.

Spring was the time that I began to think about playing baseball. Time to get out my old field glove, rub a little oil in the palm to soften it up and practice a few throws. After Emil left the farm when I was about ten, there was no one to play catch with me. . Daddy was busy with farm work and besides he was already fifty-six years old when I was ten. So I threw a rubber ball against the side of the barn for practice. Sometimes I would ride my bicycle out to Doswell and play baseball with the Carter boys but most of the baseball was played at school during recess.

Easter was a big day in our spring activities. Only later when we had a car did Mama and I go to church on Easter. Usually, all of my brothers and sisters and their families came up from Richmond for Easter. Of course, Mama cooked a big meal but all of the girls, my sisters as well as girlfriends and wives, helped also. For us children the big event was the Easter egg hunt. We prayed there would be good weather so we could hold it outside. If it was rainy, then the hunt was inside, still a lot of fun. Preparations for the big day started the week before Easter. Mama had been saving egg shells for a month. These were washed and carefully trimmed so that about three-quarters of the shell was intact. On Easter day all of the children helped to prepare the eggs. We put candy corn and jelly beans in the shells and then sealed them with a piece of white tissue glued over the opening. The glue was made of flour and water. Of course, there were also hard-boiled eggs which we dyed various colors and patterns. All of these were hidden later by the adults for the children to find.

The only thing that would stop the outside Easter egg hunt was rain. In that case, all the children were kept in the kitchen while the eggs were hidden by the adults. Eggs could be hidden behind pictures, in flower pots, in the chair cushions, the bookcase or any other clever place. Usually one bedroom was also designated a hiding place and there even more ingenious places were used. Eggs were put in dresser drawers or pockets of hanging clothes or behind wall pictures.

When all the eggs were hidden, the children raced out of the kitchen with their baskets and gathered as many eggs as they could. When I was five or six and still believed in the "bunny rabbit," Mama bought Easter baskets for us and set them out in the living room near the fireplace for us to find in the morning. Each typically contained one chocolate bunny, some jelly beans, a few of the hard candy eggs and a couple of the yellow marshmellow baby chicks. They were all nestled in a basket of green cellophane grass. Although I dearly loved chocolate, I always saved the chocolate bunny last because I hated to bite off his head.

Oh, but there was work to be done, too, in the spring. Daddy had to do the plowing using either the mule, Molly, or our horse, Albert. It was hard work. Some of the fields like the one next to the barn were on a slight hill. The furrows had to be cut in to minimize washing. For planting, we had a horse-drawn two-wheel machine with a long box between the wheels which held whatever seed was to be planted. A number of tubes extended down from the seed box which deposited the seeds at regular intervals into the soft earth. The spacing of the seeds dropped could be adjusted, setting distance between "hills." The width of the rows planted was set by shutting off a number of the tubes. The spacing between the active tubes dropping the seed then set the spacing between the rows. It was actually a pretty clever machine and a great labor saver over planting by hand.

We always had at least a couple of milk cows which gave us milk almost all year. In the spring the cows eagerly grazed in the pasture after a long winter without any green grass. Green onions are the first things that come up in the spring. Naturally, the cows loved them. The result was that all the milk in the spring had a strong onion taste. I never liked it, but Mama said, "Drink your milk. It's just as good for you with that onion flavor. You'll get used to it in a few days. Before long, all the onions in the pasture will be gone and the milk will have its regular taste." I drank it, but I never liked it or got used to it.

Mama made a type of cheese from the milk which she called "smearcase." The name comes from the German word *schmierkase,* meaning a type of spreadable cheese: *schmieren,* to smear + *kase,* cheese. Mama had a number of recipes that were German. I think she learned these while she and Daddy lived in Maryland. That part of Maryland is not too far from the Pennsylvania Dutch country and no doubt some of our dishes were influenced by the Pennsylvania Dutch. To make the smearcase, she used sour milk, not buttermilk, which she heated until it was lukewarm and turned into thick clabber. This was allowed to cool which separated the milk curds from the whey. The whey, "liquid," was drained off leaving only the milk curds which were like cottage cheese. To preserve the smearcase she put the soggy curds in a piece of cheesecloth and hung it outdoors on the clothesline to dry. The dry smearcase could be kept for days and then reconstituted with a little fresh milk when it was served. We had this type of soft cheese throughout all the warm months of the year. It was particularly tasty combined with fresh vegetables in a salad.

Daddy always saved seeds from the preceding year for planting the new crops. Garden seedlings, like tomato and green pepper, were started in paperboard boxes which he kept in the kitchen window sill. When they had grown some, and the soil outside warmed a bit, he transferred them to a wooden box set in the ground and covered by an old glass window. The sun warmed the soil and the seedlings grew fast. When they had grown to four or five inches tall, he transferred them to the garden. As the months warmed up, we had our first green vegetables: such as leaf lettuce, pea pods and radishes from our garden. They were a welcome change after the long winter of canned and dried foods. By summer we would have a full range of vegetables. From our garden we would get sweet corn, tomatoes, string beans, beets, yellow squash, Irish potatoes and peppers. Daddy always planted additional patches of potatoes, both Irish and sweet, as well as sweet corn in one of the nearby fields. We needed lots of vegetables for summer eating as well as for Mama to can for winter. Things like pumpkins, cantaloupes and watermelons were planted on the sandy flats below the house—-they needed lots of room. Our strawberry patch was also planted on the flats.

Of course, we had also some fruit trees: apple, cherry, peach, pear and plum. One of the earliest fruits available was gooseberries. We had two bushes in our garden. The gooseberries were about one quarter to one half inch in size, yellowish red in color with vein markings. They grew two to a branch along with a husky thorn. Whenever I picked them, I always got several sticks on my fingers. But it was worth it because Mama would make a delicious gooseberry pie. Gooseberries have a very tart taste if eaten raw. Of course, Mama added sugar or honey to the pie and it was a real treat. Sometimes she made preserves from them, too. With the variety of vegetables and fruits we raised plus the basic crops of corn, wheat and hay, no wonder it seemed there was little time for play.

By the time we got into the month of May, the weather was warm enough to change into lighter clothes for school. It was also time to change from those lace-up boots that I had worn all fall and winter into a pair of tennis shoes. Those tennis shoes felt so light on my feet. On a really warm day, I would slip off my shoes and go barefooted once I was on our dirt road. There were places on the road that were very sandy and that warm sand on my bare feet felt so good. That's when I knew that the free days of summer were not far off. Walking home with my shoes across my shoulders was such a good feeling. Of course, before I came out of the woods and reached the open fields of our farm, I stopped and put my shoes back on. I suspect Mama knew I had been barefooted when I washed my feet in the bathtub before going to bed. She often cautioned me about going barefooted because she was afraid I might step on some sharp object. There were plenty of opportunities to get hurt on the farm.

Daddy always kept three or four hives of honey bees to supply us with honey. In order to work around the bees and not get stung, he had a protective cloth headpiece, sort of a helmet with a screen in the front so he could see what he was doing. This helmet came down over his neck and shoulders so the bees couldn't get to any bare skin. He also wore a pair of long gloves to protect his hands. Of course, bee work was always done with long pants and a long sleeve shirt. He also had a "smoker" which was used if he needed to move a lot of the bees out of the way to extract the honey. The "smoker" looked a bit like a coffee pot with a bellows on the back. Daddy loaded it with burning rags and when he pumped the back handle, it would send out smoke from a spout on the front. I used to watch him extract the frames from the hives all loaded with honey. I never got too close; I had been stung a few times and remembered how it felt. I loved to get a piece of the honey, comb and all, and suck on it while I was playing. The honey was a nice supplement to the jellies and jams that Mama preserved. Mama also used honey in baking as a substitute for sugar. And there was always that cup of tea, sweetened with honey, to compliment a piece of cake or a few cookies.

On spring nights we could hear the bullfrogs bellowing all the way from that swampy place off the southeast corner of our farm. It was about a mile away, but if you stepped outside you could easily hear them. The breeding time for the bullfrogs was in the spring. They were bellowing in hopes of getting a response from an interested female frog. We were not interested in the mating habits of the bullfrogs, but it was a time we could go and catch a few of those delicious frog legs to eat. After it was completely dark, we donned rubber boots and packed along a kerosene lantern and a couple flashlights. There was an old rowboat at the edge of the swamp which we used once we bailed out the water. The swamp was shallow, so we poled the boat amongst the trees and stopped often to determine the direction of the nearest bellowing bullfrog. The lantern was on the stern seat of the rowboat and we used our flashlights to try and spot a bullfrog. If we could get within about eight feet of a bullfrog, we could stab him with our gig. The gig was a sort of two-pronged spear with a long handle. The bullfrog would be submerged, except for his head, and it was tricky to get close enough to gig him before he jumped away. These were big frogs, typically about six inches long, and very wary. If we were lucky, we might gig a half dozen in an hour. Well after midnight, we would trod home with our catch. Only the hind legs were saved for Mama to cook the next day. She breaded them and fried them just as you would chicken. The meat was very tender and even tasted a bit like chicken. They were a tasty addition to our usual food.

School finished the last of May. So for me, summer began the first of June when school was over. What a wonderful feeling to know that I had three months of freedom ahead of me. There was work to be done but also time for play. Summer was coming—what joy!

9

Summer

Short pants, light shirt, straw hat and barefooted—that was the combination that meant summer. Of course, that was for play; a different outfit was worn for serious work in the fields. I was light skinned with red hair and plenty of freckles. I had to be a little careful of the sun. But, oh, how good it was to be up early and hear the birds singing and the cows mooing in the barn. There's nothing like being awakened by a rooster crowing his welcome to the rising sun. Even doing my morning chores, like tending the chickens, was a pleasure.

Hay Harvest

This was the time for bringing in the first crop of hay. Daddy had a horse-drawn mower which he used to cut the hay. We also had a hay rake, also drawn by a horse, which collected the hay and then could be dumped by the operator into long rows. I used to like to ride the hay rake, guide the horse and then throw the lever which raised the tongs to dump the hay. The hay was left in the rows to dry thoroughly. That took a couple days of good sunshine. In fact, rain while the hay was in rows, could mean the loss of the whole crop unless we got out there and spread the hay to prevent mildew. If that was done, then it had to be raked up again into rows or else a lot of hand work with pitchforks. If we had been lucky and didn't have rain, then we divided the rows, using our pitchforks, and piled the hay in small hay stacks. While watching the skies for rain, we next had to haul the hay to the barn for storage. My job was to drive the wagon alongside the piles of hay and Daddy would pitch it up onto the wagon. I walked about on it to pack it down and then drove the horses forward to the next piles. One day Daddy pitched up a bundle of hay and along with it was a big black snake. I was always afraid of snakes so I yelled out and jumped off the other side of the wagon to the ground. Daddy wanted to know what was the matter. I explained. I wouldn't go back up on the wagon until Daddy got up on the hay and pitched the snake down. The snake had probably been under the pile of hay where it was nice and cool. After that, I watched carefully as Daddy pitched up hay on the wagon and was always a little afraid I might again encounter a snake.

Once we were fully loaded we headed for the barn. I drove the wagon into the center of the barn and unhooked the team. Then I took them around to the side of the barn and hooked them to a heavy rope that came out of the barn through a pulley. This rope went through a series of pulleys and connected to the hay lift which was the shape of an inverted "U." The hay lift came down from the apex of the barn roof and Daddy pushed it down into the hay on the wagon. The hay lift took a big bite of the hay and was hoisted up to the hay loft by the team connected to the rope outside. My job was to drive the team straight out from the barn at sufficient speed so that the lift struck the track at the top of barn and then switched onto a track carrying the load of hay to the rear of the barn. At that point, Daddy dropped the load of hay by pulling on two lines he had attached to the hay lift. When properly done, it was a marvelous operation and it only took four or five lifts to empty the wagon. But often times the team was tired and would not go fast enough even with my yelling and whipping them. When that happened, the hay lift jammed up in the roof of the barn and failed to switch to the track. That meant the hay lift load would have to be dropped back on the wagon and the whole procedure repeated.

My Daddy used some harsh language on me at those times because it was my job to make the team pull hard and fast. I hated that job. But I know it was frustrating to Daddy, too. After a few aborted lifts we would get all the hay off the wagon and be ready for another trip to the hay field. It was hard work.

Corn Thinning

By early summer it was time to do the corn thinning. Our horse-drawn corn planter dropped three to five kernels of corn in every hill. That was to protect against seeds that didn't sprout. However, it always seemed to me that at least three or four corn plants sprouted. Daddy said that unless the extra corn plants were removed, the corn would not mature with robust ears. So, my instructions were to remove all except two plants. It was a back-breaking job to bend down and pull out those extra corn shoots from every hill. The corn plant has roots that spread out just under the soil and often entangled the roots of the other plant. So, when you thinned the corn, you had to pull out the unwanted plants carefully and then press down the soil around the remaining ones. Even when you got experienced, it took a little time. Sometimes my niece and nephew, Gretchen and Roger, were visiting for a week up from Richmond and they helped. Although it was a hot job, it was a novelty to them. However, the novelty wore off in a couple hours. We usually worked in the morning and then had a nice lunch and maybe a trip down to the river for a swim in the afternoon. But when I had to work alone those corn rows seem to go on forever. Whenever we worked in the fields, we took a quart Mason jar of water wrapped in a wet burlap sack, which we parked in the shade at the edge of the woods. The wet burlap would evaporate in the hot weather cooling the water. It was a simple and effective method of getting cool drinking water. Thinning corn was hard work and one of the jobs I never liked.

A Sunday afternoon swim in the North Anna River.
(l to r) Emil, Latimer Watkins, Margaret, Robert,
Evelyn, Roger, LeRoy, Janice, Gretchen.

Because of my light complexion (red hair and freckles), I usually had to wear a long sleeve shirt and always my straw hat to keep from getting sunburned. There was no sun protection lotions in those days and a couple hours of that hot July sun could leave me looking like a boiled lobster. Oh yes, many times I did get sunburned and it was really painful. On the bad burns I would be covered with dollar-sized blisters. My face was splotched with freckles in summer. How I wished I could have that uniform tan of some of my playmates!

The River

The North Anna River ran just beyond the east boundary of our farm. In spring it often flooded and was a roaring muddy river with logs and tree branches sweeping by. We used to walk down and watch the cascading water from the safey of the high bank. Often the river would flood so bad that it overflowed its banks and we had to watch from afar. By summer, it was a docile stream with clear water about four feet deep at most. At our swimming hole the river was only about fifty feet wide. With help from all of my older brothers and sisters, I learned to swim at an early age. Non-swimmers were helped across the channel, the deep part, to a sandy beach on the far side. From there they could wade into the shallow part and practice the "dog paddle," as we called it. From the "dog paddle" we advanced to overhand strokes and backstroke. Boys and girls bathing suits were all the same: one piece Navy blue wool jersey. Even the grown men wore tops to their trunks. It was considered unseemly for men to go swimming with a bare chest (and against the law in city pools). For a little variation, sometimes a man's bathing suit would have a white top with the standard Navy blue wool jersey shorts. Women's' suits were all one piece wool jersey but they did have some color variations: blue, purple or perhaps burgundy.

About fifty feet off the path that led down through the woods to the river was what we called the "Indian spring." We often stopped there for a cooling drink of the most delicious water. The water poured out of a mossy slope into a rock basin about one foot in diameter. The rock was in the shape of a rough bowl. The story we were told was that the Indians had ground out the rock to form a bowl to catch the water. We knew there had been Indians on the land of our farm because we found numerous Indian arrowheads. Of course, if the spring had been running for hundreds of years the water itself could have worn away the rock. We liked the story of the Indians better so the spring was always referred to as the "Indian spring."

We found ample evidence on our farm that there had been Indians on the land years ago. It was very common to find arrowheads of all sizes and shapes on that large sandy field below the farmhouse that we called the "flats." This was where we grew our watermelons, cantaloupes and strawberries. They thrived in the sandy soil. The sweetest watermelons were those small green colored round ones we called "sugar babies." They were no larger than a basketball and almost perfectly round. After picking we kept them cool in our spring house. You could tell if you had a really ripe one when you plunged the knife into it. If it started to split as you plunged in your knife, then it was going to be a really good one.

Often we would find arrowheads on the flats when we were plowing to prepare for planting or when we were harvesting. Legend had it that this area had been a lakebed in earlier times. It could have been fed from a branch of the North Anna River if the course of the river had been different several hundred years ago. Perhaps the Indians had hunted waterfowl if there had been a lake. We found an occasional arrowhead elsewhere on the farm but not near as many as we did on this sandy plain. Over the years we collected a whole shoe box of arrowheads. Many times I made bows of green hickory limbs and tried to fashion arrows using the arrowheads we had found. These were mostly dismal failures because I could never get a good attachment of the arrowhead to the stick I was using as the arrow shaft. The Indians split the end of the shaft and then lashed it to the arrowhead with narrow strips of deer hide. My attempts at "arrow building" were not successful but I still had a lot of fun running through the woods pretending I was an Indian.

Going to the river was a treat after a day of working in the hot corn fields or hauling hay to the barn. The near side of the river had a high bank so Daddy had installed some steep wooden steps, almost like a ladder. On the far side of the river was that sandy "beach" about forty feet in depth. As long as I can remember it was called "Berta's Beach" after the wife of my oldest brother, Randolph. Alberta was not much of a water person and used to stay on that strip of sand while the rest of us played in the water. There was also a sunken tree in the main swimming hole with two limbs projecting out of the water at an angle providing a place to climb up and dive into the water.

On Sundays, when my grown brothers and sisters came up from Richmond with their girlfriends, boyfriends and spouses, it was always a big deal to make a trek to the river for a swim. The walk was down the hill from the farmhouse, across the "flats" and a short distance into the woods. (I guess it must have been no more than a mile.) How refreshing a swim was before we returned to a supper of fried chicken, biscuits and fresh vegetables from the garden—all washed down by lots of cold tea. Not ice tea, because we seldom had any ice, but it was good and cool from sitting in the cool water of our spring house. On special occasions, when we had fruit or berries, maybe strawberries or peaches, we would make ice cream. That required a lot of preparation and planning. It meant that we had to go to Campbell's store on Saturday afternoon and buy a block of ice, about 25 pounds, wrap it in several layers of burlap and bring it back to the farm by horse and wagon. Then the ice would be further wrapped and put in the spring house. By Sunday a lot of it had melted but there was still enough to make five-gallons of hand turned ice-cream. Mama made the mix and put it into the shiny container which was in the center of the wooden ice cream mixer. It was hand cranked, of course. All of the kids took turns at the crank with the promise of an extra large bowl of ice cream when it was finished. It was cranked until it got so stiff we could hardly turn it. Then it was packed with more rock salt and ice and put in the spring house until we had our supper.

Each summer Gretchen and Roger, both my age, would spend a week or two on the farm. It was great fun to have them and a real change from their city life in Richmond. One day Gretchen, Roger and I decided it would be fun to have a boat at the river. We had never built a boat but we were sure we could. Daddy gave us some planks and we began laying out the boat in back of the barn. We didn't want it too big because then we couldn't handle it. It needed to be large enough to hold two of us. When we finally settled on the dimensions and shape, we sawed the planks to make the sides. But we couldn't bend the side planks much and the shape ended up more like a triangle than the typical boat outline. We nailed planks crosswise to make the bottom. When we had the boat assembled, we noticed a lot of cracks which signaled significant leaks. We found some tar in the barn and used that along with strips of cloth to plug as many of the cracks as we could. The next day we set it on my wood hauling wagon and set off for the river. Once we reached the woods on the way to the river we had to carry it. It was a job and we had quite a bit of tar on us by the time we got to the river. We launched the boat with great expectations and immediately saw that we had a lot of leaks. We had heard that a wooden boat would swell once it was in the water and stop most of the leaks; so we weren't too worried. We wanted to try out our boat and didn't have time to wait for the wood to swell. So we launched it and found that one person could ride in it for a short distance before it had to be beached and emptied of the water. We figured that would be all right. Roger suggested we tow the boat up stream and then take turns riding it down. The river was low so we could wade in it with water at our waist. We trudged upstream for a long time. At one point I was wading and looking up at a buzzard circling lazily in the sky and I stepped into a hole that was over my head. I slipped under water leaving my straw hat floating on top. It was only for an instant but it gave me a scare. I came up coughing and spitting water. Roger and Gretchen thought it was comical and were laughing and pointing to my straw hat as it floated downstream. I recovered my hat and was a little more careful about holes after that.

Gretchen paddles our homemade boat on the river.

Waiting for the Sunday company to arrive. (l to r)
Emil, Mama, Daddy, LeRoy. Circa 1937.

We must have gone upriver a couple miles when we decided we were tired of towing the boat and turned around to begin the float down river. We took turns riding in the boat, one at a time. The boat leaked so much that we had to stop every five minutes or so and beach it to empty out the water. What an adventure the three of us had! By the time we returned to our old swimming hole we each had a lot of tar on our legs and arms. I knew that was going to be hard to get off. We tied up the boat at the swimming hole and trudged home. We were excited about the great river float we had taken but were concerned about Mama and Daddy's reaction. We decided we would not tell them about going so far up the river and about my slipping into the hole. But the tar evidence was not something we could hide. When we got back home, we went first to the barn and got kerosene and rubbed it on our arms and legs to remove some of the tar. We had gotten some sunburn and that kerosene made us sting something awful. We cleaned up the best we could and then went to the house to have Mama and Daddy give us a stern lecture on how hard it was to get tar off of anything. Boy, we already knew that! Actually, they weren't too hard on us. I guess they figured we had learned a lot and obviously had a grand time from all the excited comments we made. We played with our boat most of the summer until a heavy rain caused flood conditions on the river and our boat was swept away. The leaking had never improved. I guess it just didn't swell up like we had heard it would.

Summer Games

Roger and Gretchen were my favorite playmates because they were close to my age. They were children of my oldest sister, Janice. None of my other brothers or sisters had any children my age. My brother, Emil, played with me some but he was four years older and not interested in many of the playtimes I liked. So I really looked for the times when Roger and Gretchen came to the farm. Of course, they came to the farm about every other Sunday. After supper on summer evenings we had a lot of fun playing in the yard while the adults were sitting and talking. About twilight the bats would be flying about catching insects. We would get small pebbles and throw them up high when a bat was flying by and watch him dive after it until he discovered that it was not something to eat. Catching "lighting bugs," or fireflies, as Northerners called them, in a glass jar was another pastime. We also played a game we called "Annie Over." We got on opposite side of the house and had a rubber ball like a tennis ball to throw over the roof. First, we yelled, "Annie Over," and then we threw the ball over the house. The object was to fool the person on the other side of the house as to where you were throwing the ball. The receiver did his best to catch the ball. He then called, "Annie Over," and tried to throw the ball over the roof where he thought the other player was not. The game became increasingly difficult as it neared darkness. Funny, how a simple game like that kept our interest for a long time. We also played hide and go seek. One person was chosen "it" to begin the game. That person would close his eyes and stand at "home" which was usually a tree in the yard. He would loudly count out to a hundred by tens while all the other kids ran and hid. At the count of one hundred, he would yell, "Coming! Ready or not!" Then he would try both to guard his "home" and to find the other kids that were hiding. Those hiding would try to run to "home" without getting tagged by the one called "it." If all succeeded in getting "home" without getting tagged, then "it" had to serve again and the process was repeated. However, the first person to get tagged, had to serve at the home next time and he was "it." All of the outside games involved a lot of running around which is why we kids probably slept so good at night.

Threshing Time

Wheat that was planted in the winter was ready for harvesting in early July. By July each stalk of wheat was headed with plump grains ready for gathering. In our part of the country there were no combines as were used in the great wheat areas of the Midwest. The combine cuts the wheat and shells out the grains as it moves along in the field, a combined operation. Hence the name"combine." We did it the old fashioned way. We had a machine called a binder for harvesting the grain in the field. It was drawn by two horses and had a seat for an operator. There was a long mower blade with many trapezoidal blades that shunted back forth as the horses pulled the binder. This part was just like the mower we had for cutting hay. Then there was a reel about four feet in diameter that rotated as the machine moved and it struck the standing grain as it was cut and knocked it back on a conveyor curtain—all the stalks lying in the same direction. The conveyor curtain carried the grain stalks and collected them in a bundle. On a regular timing, a hook shaped device would rise out of the bowels of the machine and wrap a length of binder twine around the bundle of wheat sheaves and tie it. I was always amazed at the complexity of the machine and the reliability of each tied bundle of wheat. This version of the binder had been invented by McCormick and perfected over the years. The model we had was first introduced in the 1880's and had changed little from that time. Later versions were pulled by a tractor.

As I drove the binder I had nothing to do, up to this point, except to guide the horses and keep them out of the standing wheat. When three or four bundles of the wheat had been tied and collected on the tray of the binder, I would throw a lever and dump the bundles on the ground. A good operator dropped them so as to form a series of rows across the field. Daddy then collected them with his pitchfork and tossed them into a shock. The shocks were made into a sort of cone shape to hopefully shed most of the rain while the wheat dried. This was another time when a long rainy spell could doom the wheat crop by soaking the wheat and causing it to mildew. Weather was such a factor in farming. Now while the wheat was drying in the field, we waited for the threshing machine to come to our farm.

Neighbors always helped each other at threshing time. The Cannon family lived on the adjoining farm and they always helped us at threshing time and we did the same for them. Daddy knew a few days ahead when the threshing machine would come our way. The man that owned the machine went from farm to farm on the same route each year so it was predictable a few days ahead when he would show up at our place. I never understood why, but it seemed the threshing machine often came on the fourth of July. Of course, holidays didn't mean much on a farm, except perhaps for Christmas, Thanksgiving and Easter. The threshing machine was pulled by a Fordson tractor and could be heard a mile away. It usually came by way of the flats, that part of our farm that stretched down toward the North Anna River. From our farmhouse on the hill, I could hear and see it coming when it was far away. This was an exciting time: the operation of the thresher and the fact that two of the Cannon men, Manley and Leonard, were there to help us. It was also a very hard workday that required us to work very fast. Daddy had to pay for the time the thresher was at our place so it was important that we get the job done in one day. Manley and Leonard were two of the bachelor men in the Cannon family. They had a younger brother, and three sisters: Lucille in high school, Mozelle (grown) and Mary who had a daughter, Marjory, my age.

Manley and Leonard Cannon brought over their team and wagon to help in hauling the wheat to the thresher. The thresher was set up near the barn where the straw could be exhausted into a convenient pile. The Fordson tractor was unhitched and put in position to power the thresher through a belt drive. I was fascinated by all of this machinery and the associated noise—so different from all our horse drawn machinery. Once the thresher was positioned we went to the fields with the wagons to bring in the wheat. Emil was stationed at the thresher to bag the grain as it came out of the chute of the thresher. I drove our wagon and Daddy pitched up the bundles of wheat until we had a load. Then we headed for the barn and the thresher. When we were going in, the Cannon team was heading out to the field. That way we could keep a steady supply of wheat in the thresher. The wagon was driven alongside the thresher and the bundles of wheat tossed into the chute. The chute had a series of rotating blades which cut the twine on each bundle and then the wheat was carried into the machine on a conveyor belt. I never knew exactly how the grains of wheat were removed from their stalks, but miraculously wheat grains poured out the pipe on the side of the machine into burlap sacks. Part of the time I traded jobs with Emil. Then I had the duty to hold the sacks at that outlet pipe and move them quickly out of the way when they were full. That was the dirtiest and noisiest part of the whole operation. The air was filled with dust and chaff. It was hot as blazes and the noise of the thresher and tractor was deafening, but I thought it was really exciting.

We worked from early morning until noon when we stopped for dinner—our mid-day meal. The previous day we had set up tables in the shade using planks on sawhorses. These were covered with a checkered oilcloth tablecloth. Mama, sometimes with the help of one of the Cannon girls, had prepared a real feast for all the help. (Of course, in earlier days before all the other children left the farm, Mama had help from my sisters and my brothers helped Daddy with the threshing. But now, only Emil and I were left to help and in a year or two he also was off to Richmond. That left me, the last of eight children, to help with the threshing.

Even the thresher operator joined us for the noon meal. Typically, we had lots of fried chicken, mashed potatoes and gravy, fresh vegetables, hot biscuits, gallons of cold tea, and maybe even a cake or pie. If watermelons were ripe at that time, a couple of them which had been chilled in the spring house would top off the meal. After the meal the men sat around and talked for a while and Emil and I stretched out on the grass under those black walnut trees in our yard. I fell asleep instantly and it seemed only minutes until Daddy called, "LeRoy, it's time to hitch up the team and get another load of wheat from the field."

The threshing was a dirty, hot, tiring job for all of us. Besides being dirty, my ears would be ringing for hours from all the noise if I had spent much time at the thresher loading the sacks of grain. My muscles were stiff and sore from handling those bags of grain at the thresher and from hauling in the shocks of wheat from the field with the horse and wagon. We all hoped that we could finish by late afternoon so Emil and I could go down to the river and take a swim. A dive in that cool river would wash away all that dirt and chaff and leave us refreshed. Usually it worked out that way unless there was a breakdown in some part of the threshing machine or the Fordson tractor. If we finished a couple hours before dark, then the thresher operator would hook up the tractor and tow the thresher off of our farm headed for his next stop. When it was all done, we knew we had grain for the chickens, seed for the winter planting and grain we would turn into flour, enough to last us until next year.

Night Sounds

One of the pleasures of summer was listening to the night sounds as I lay in my bed in that little alcove on the second level of the farmhouse. With the windows open there was a virtual symphony of sounds. Bullfrogs in the swamp way away in the woods gave a melodious bass of "Brr—rung, brr—rung, brr—rung." Then there was a big horned owl that called, "Hoo—hoo—hoo." This owl had a favorite place in a big cedar tree down on the flats of our farm a long ways from our house, but his calling could be clearly heard. It was a spooky call, but one that I never tired of hearing. I saw him occasionally sitting on a limb of that cedar tree that we passed on the way down to the swimming hole at the river. The tuffs of feathers on each side of his head resembled horns, hence the name. Of course, owls are nocturnal and seldom move about in the daytime. He would just sit there with his big eyes glaring down at me and moving his head from side to side. Seldom did he fly off his perch. Occasionally at night, there would also be a piercing scream from a screech owl, as we called it. This owl made a cry like the scream of a woman being attacked or suddenly frightened. It was enough to make chills run up my spine. I never liked to hear that sound. Much more comforting was the study hum and buzz of the cicadas, which we called locusts, in the trees in our yard. I often went to sleep listening to their droning in the background. There are a number of different types of cicadas. The most famous are the periodical; they return every thirteen or seventeen years, depending on the brood. But there are other types called "Dog Days Cicadas" that appear every year in the "dog days of summer"—- July and August. Those must have been the types we had on the farm because I remember them every summer with their drone and hum.

Of all the night sounds, the one I liked the best was the song of the Whippoorwill. You seldom see or hear this bird in the daytime. They are a robin-sized bird about the color of dried leaves. They make their nest on the ground, usually in some dense, protected place, often under a bush. They become active about dusk when they go after night flying insects which they take back to their babies or their nest-sitting mate. When it begins to get dark, you can hear them for the first time with their plaintive call of "Whip poor Will, whip-poor- Will, whip- poor-Will." As they hunt for insects they continue their call on into the night. Sometimes they will follow this call with something that sounds like, "O whirr-r, whirro! O whirr-r, whirro!" Many times I fell asleep listening to this chorus of bullfrogs, owls, locusts and my favorite, the Whippoorwill.

Berries and Chiggers

Wild blackberries grew along creek banks, fence lines and other places where there was sun. When they were ripe, Mama would suggest we go and pick some and she would promise to make a blackberry cobbler for supper. Now blackberries have some of the most tenacious thorns of any berry. The biggest berries come from the healthiest bushes and that means the ones with the meanest thorns. Our outfit for picking berries was usually long sleeves, long pants and a hat. This was pretty uncomfortable in the middle of the summer but necessary to try to protect us from those nasty thorns and chiggers. Chiggers are tiny mites about the size of a period on a printed page. When they bite, a welt is left and there is intense itching which lasts for a couple days. If you only got a bite or so on your arms or legs, that wouldn't be so bad. But chiggers don't operate like that. Typically if you went blackberry picking and got any chiggers, you'd get a lot of chigger bites. Furthermore, they liked to bite in the most sensitive places on your body. Favorite places were where your underclothes were tight around your legs and abdomen. The problem was that we didn't have anything to relieve the itching. The best procedure was to come home and immediately take a bath with strong soap. Well, most times we would forget about the chiggers until bedtime and then it was too late. Besides, who would take a cold bath in the middle of the day. Even so, that blackberry cobbler of Mama's for supper made it all worthwhile.

Flour and Cornmeal

In late August we always made a trip to the Ashland Flour Mill to take the wheat and corn that would be ground into flour and cornmeal. By that time the wheat that was threshed in July would be dried out and ready to be made into flour. Corn was another matter. The current year's corn would not be harvested until late September and still needed time to thoroughly dry. So we had to use corn left over from the previous year. We had a hand cranked corn sheller that was really a two man operation. One person fed the ears of corn into the top while the other cranked a sort of drum with knobs on it. When the corn ears were nice and dry, the machine did a good job of shelling the grains from the cob. You could only feed in a couple of ears at a time, so it was a slow process to shell a quantity of corn. We needed several burlap bags of shelled corn for the trip to the mill. That was a job Daddy and I did the week before we planned to go to the mill.

"Well, today doesn't look to be too hot. I think we'll go down to the mill. LeRoy, you can take your fishing rod," Daddy announced at breakfast.

The trip to the mill was always interesting for me. It would be a long day riding in the wagon loaded with bags of wheat and corn. It was certainly something different from a day on the farm. After breakfast we loaded the wagon with the sacks of wheat and corn and hitched up Albert, our horse, and Molly, the mule.

"Here's your lunch," Mama said, passing up a sack of sandwiches and a quart Mason jar of cold tea. "LeRoy, when you get to the mill, find a shady place on the edge of the pond and put this tea in the water. Maybe it will be a little cool for lunch. And don't forget to keep your straw hat on or you'll burn to a crisp." Mama was always cautioning me about sunburn which was a good idea because we didn't have anything to prevent it and I surely did burn and freckle.

We waved good-bye and began the long trip. The Ashland Flour Mill was five miles south of Doswell on US Route #1. Add the two miles from our farm to Doswell and we had a trip of about seven miles that would take us three to four hours. US #1 was a four lane highway that ran from Florida to Maine. We had to be extra careful with our horse drawn wagon. Fortunately, there was a good shoulder on the side of the road most of the way and that's where we drove the wagon. Still it was a dangerous route. US #1 had a lot of trucks because it was the primary road from Richmond to Washington and points north and south.

By midmorning it was getting hot, so we stopped at Little River to give the team a drink and to let them rest a bit. After another mile or so we began the long descent toward the South Anna River where the mill was located. It was close off the highway. The river had a dam at the mill and a sluice which provided the water to turn the enormous waterwheel.

"Looks like some others are ahead of us. We may have to wait awhile," Daddy commented as we pulled the wagon off the highway and into the parking area around the mill.

"Can I go in the mill and watch them grinding the flour while we wait?" I asked.

"Better wait until I tie the horses. I'll go in with you. You have to stay out of the way. Those fellas are mighty busy and don't have time to look out for someone just wandering around. Plenty places to get hurt in there." Daddy knew how I was fascinated by all the belt drives, pulleys and rotating power takeoffs that the mill had. I was about to wander off to look at the mill pond and the water wheel when he reminded me that we had to unload our wagon.

"LeRoy, get that flatbed cart over by the mill door and bring it over here to the wagon. That'll be easier than carrying these sacks of grain over to the mill."

We unloaded the sacks of wheat and corn and rolled them over to the platform at the entrance of the mill. The miller came out to tag our bags. He was covered with a dusting of the white flour. His cap and clothes were white with flour as was his face, hands and hair. He looked like he was wearing a white mask. Even his eyebrows and eyelashes were white with the flour.

"I see you brung your helper along today", he winked to Daddy, motioning toward me.

" Yeah. But he's mostly interested in fishing in the pond and watching all the wheels go round in the mill." Daddy laughed, looking sideways at me. I knew Daddy was kidding.

"It's gonna be a while, Mr. Day. We're backed up. Seems like everybody wants their flour just now," the miller explained.

"Daddy, I think I'll go fishing now before we have our lunch. I'll get to see things inside the mill when he's grinding our stuff."

At that time the Ashland Flour Mill was perhaps seventy years old. It was located on the South Ana River where the river fell quite a bit. A dam was built at this spot and the mill was located just below the dam. The resulting mill pond served as the power source for the mill. The mill had one of the old style massive wooden water wheels. It was the so-called "overshot type." That meant the water was directed by a millrace or sluice to strike the water wheel near its top, fill the wooden buckets around the periphery and cause the wheel to rotate. Water in the sluice could be controlled by a gate which could be operated by a person inside the mill. A series of belts and pulleys took the power from the waterwheel and turned the millstones grinding the grain. The Ashland Flour Mill had been in operation since the Civil War and is still in operation, except that now it is run by electricity.

I thought the mill pond was a special place to fish. The water was clear and you could see sunlight glinting off the sunfish as they came in to investigate your bait. It was different from the North Anna River back near our farm, which was often muddy. A few red worms from under some rocks along the bank was all the bait I needed. Of course, I had to throw back any fish I caught; we had no way of keeping them while we made the long trip home. Besides, the fish were pretty small but I suppose you could still call them "pan size." This day was slow fishing. I only got a few bites and caught two small sunfish. Anyway, it was fun. I enjoyed the peace and quiet, sitting on the bank under that big maple tree. The creaking of the water wheel and all that water sloshing made for a restful time. I was jarred out of my daydreaming by Daddy calling that it was lunch time.

"Did you put the tea in the shade somewhere?" Daddy asked. Only then did I remember that Mama had told me to do that.

"No, I forgot it. It's under the seat in the wagon where I put it." Daddy looked a little disgusted but I guess it wasn't the first time one of his sons had failed to follow instructions.

"Well, LeRoy, I guess we won't have cool tea with our lunch. Here, pour yourself some warm tea. Next time you pay attention to what your mother told you and don't go off fishing until you've done the things you were told to do." Daddy was clearly irritated, but it soon passed as we sat on the bank of the pond under that big maple and ate our lunch.

When we had finished our lunch, we went inside the mill to see if the miller had started grinding our grain. Actually he was through grinding all our wheat but one bag. The corn had been ground and the cornmeal was there in the corner. Our flour was stacked in clean white bags against the wall. The whole atmosphere in the mill had a sort of fog of flour. The white flour dust was everywhere. Even the big belts that ran from the many pulleys had a sort of grayish tint to them.

"How do you stop the grinding when all the wheat is gone?" I shouted to the miller over the din.

He was busy loading some sacks with the freshly ground flour. He straightened up, wiped the sweat from his brow and said, " Well, we usually don't stop the grinding unless we need to clean the mill stones or if something breaks. See, that big lever over there against the wall. That opens and closes the gate in the mill race and stops water from going to the wheel. That would shut the whole mill down. We have another way. This lever up here overhead cuts out this main drive pulley and stops the turning of the mill stones. Sometimes we have to do that to get into the grist box and clean it out. That answer about all your questions, Sonny?"

"Yes, sir. But— Where does the wheat go in and the flour come out?" I was still a little unclear about the whole operation.

"You watch me. I'm gonna put in this last bag of your wheat."

The miller hoisted up the sack of wheat and poured it into the hopper in the top of the grist box that surrounded the rotating mill stones. Then he stooped down to attach one of the white flour sacks to the outlet at the bottom of the grist box.

"Your flour is coming out right now into that sack. Got it straight?" The miller winked to Daddy.

"You'd better let this man get on to his work, LeRoy. We can start loading our stuff into the wagon. It's time we got on the road," Daddy said.

Payment to the miller was a portion of the grain we brought; there was no exchange of money. That was the practice of many services offered to the farmer. The miller sold the flour and cornmeal to others thereby gaining the money he needed for his expenses.

It was mid-afternoon by the time we loaded up and started the long trek back home. A trip to the mill was always something I looked forward to each year. I lay on the sacks of flour, still warm from the grinding, and gazed upward at the lazy clouds moving overhead. Soon

I drifted off to sleep dreaming of that mill pond and catching all the fish I wanted, big ones, too.

Daddy with friends driving our farm wagon.
This was our only means of transport until we
bought our car when I was eleven in 1936.

10

Fall

Honking their way south, geese were in a long narrow wedge as they passed overhead. They were low and lighted by the setting sun as they headed for some quiet pond for the night. Perhaps they were going to some place on the South Anna River or to a quiet inlet on the Chesapeake Bay. The sight of geese migrating south always signaled fall for me. The days were definitely shorter; the mornings colder and the pace of activity on the farm changed from those warm lazy days of late summer. We were back in school and jobs on the farm centered on the late harvests and preparation for winter.

The woods surrounding our farm fields were a mixture of pines and various hardwood trees. The hardwood trees were a blaze of color this time of the year. The first colors to appear were the sumac bushes which turned a bright red. Close behind them were the dogwoods which were a slightly duller red. But the great color artists of the woods were the maples. Their leaves had colors ranging from bright yellow to a golden yellow to red, depending on the type of tree. Then there were the poplars and hickory trees with various shades of yellow and finally the oaks with their rust-yellow leaves. I saw all these types of trees on crisp fall mornings as I walked to school.

The early morning frost turned all the grass in the fields to a silvery white, Some mornings the temperature dropped a few more degrees and thin patches of ice appeared on the puddles in the road. Nature was signaling the coming cold weather. The late harvest was waiting to be reaped.

The field corn, as we called it to distinguish it from the sweet corn we ate, was feed for the animals, chickens and the source of our cornmeal. It had been left in the field to dry as much as possible before harvest. There were two ways to harvest the corn: cut the corn stalks with the ears attached and place it in shocks to dry in the field or wring off the ears of corn and leave the stalks standing for further drying. Either way it was a lot of hard work. Usually Daddy broke off the ears of corn and left the stalks standing for later cutting. I would drive the horse and wagon alongside the field and pick up the ears still in their husks and toss them in the wagon. Back at the barn we would shuck the ears and load them in the corn crib for drying and protection from mice. The corn crib was a separate little shed that was lined with a heavy wire mesh to keep out any varmints. Funny, we had mice around the barn but I don't ever remember seeing a rat. Maybe the cats kept the population in control. The standing stalks of corn had to be cut with a big heavy knife. Then they were stacked in shocks like so many teepees in rows throughout the field. When they had dried completely, we loaded them into the farm wagon for transport to the barn. They looked pretty inedible to me but the horses and cows ate them with apparent relish. Actually, the stalks of the corn are quite nutritious for the animals. All in all, the harvesting of the corn was perhaps the most labor intensive of all the crops because all of it had to be done by hand. Later, modern machines would change all of this and completely automate the whole task.

There were other crops to harvest besides the corn. Daddy always planted a couple of rows of peanuts down on the flats below the farmhouse. We usually lost a lot of them to field mice. The peanuts had to be dug up and cleaned and put someplace to dry. One of the best places to dry a small crop was on that flat roof on the room just off the kitchen. There it was safe from mice. Of course, it attracted birds and we would lose some of the crop. Once the peanuts were dried, they would keep well into the winter. Sometimes we roasted some in the oven of the wood stove for a little added flavor. They were good to eat while we were sitting around playing games or reading on a cold winter night.

We also had butter beans and black eyed peas that we allowed to remain in the field until they were dry. They had to be gathered and brought in for shelling. These beans, once dry, were stored in the cellar for use in the winter. Mama would soak them over night and then cook them as our vegetable or perhaps put them in a hearty soup. On a cold day nothing tasted better for lunch than a big bowl of homemade soup and a square of cornbread. Mama made lots of cornbread, both the regular kind made in the big black iron skillet and spoon bread baked in the oven. Spoon bread got its name because it was soft and fluffy and you could literally eat it with a spoon. Of course, Mama also made those cornbread "scratchbacks."

Now was the time to pick those delicious fall apples, pears and Concord grapes. We had grape vines on the fence on the kitchen side of our yard. Mama made grape jelly and we ate our share of them fresh off the vine. Beyond our yard facing the flats, we had a slope where we had our fruit trees. There were pears, red or sour cherries, apple, plum and peach trees. This time of the year we got pears and apples. The fall apples were Jonathan, Winesaps and the green Granny Smith. A pie made with a combination of Granny Smith and Winesap apples was my favorite. We could pick enough apples to fill a small barrel in the cellar which would give us fresh fruit until about Christmas time. Mama would make applesauce out of some. Pears wouldn't last; we let them ripen in the kitchen and ate them raw or maybe Mama would can some for desert in the winter. Sometimes she made pear preserves, a delicious spread for our home baked bread.

By late October, it was the time to harvest the pumpkins and Hubbard squash. Daddy always planted a generous patch of pumpkins and squash on that knoll just south of the barn. Both the pumpkins and squash were easy to grow and unless we had a very dry summer and fall, we always ended up with more than we could eat. Mama peeled the pumpkin , cut it into pieces and cooked it like any other vegetable. It was served with butter, salt and pepper. Pumpkin soup was another dish. Of course, some were used for pumpkin pies. The Hubbard squash was often split and baked with a little brown sugar or honey. Both the squash and pumpkin could be stored for some weeks in the cellar thereby stretching their useful time. If we really had more than we could use, we fed the excess to the hogs.

In addition to the peanuts, the last of the Irish potatoes had to be dug up and cleaned for storage. Daddy would drive the horse down each row pulling a cultivator which would unearth the potatoes. I would follow with a bucket and pick up the potatoes and dump them in a box in the wagon parked at the end of the row. We stored the potatoes in the cellar just as we did the apples. By the time we got the fruit, potatoes, root vegetables, flour, cornmeal and all of Mama's canned jars in the cellar, we had a good supply of food for the winter. That cellar had a delicious aroma from all the things stored there.

Besides harvesting those crops we grew, there were also a few wild things available in the fall. We had those two black walnut trees in our yard, another out by the barn and several in the woods beyond the lower pasture. When the walnuts first fell off the tree, they had a tough green husk. They were gathered and allowed to dry so that you could then knock off most of that husk. Then the walnuts were cracked with a hammer on a rock. We saved picking out the kernels for a later time. Getting the kernels out was a tedious job and usually reserved for an "after supper exercise" around the old kitchen table. Mama made a delicious candy with black walnuts. Besides the walnuts, if we timed it right, we could get hickory nuts after they fell and before the squirrels ate them all. There were a few hickory trees down toward the river and a couple on the way to school. The hickory nuts are smaller than walnuts and even more difficult to pick out the meat. They had a good flavor, but, between the squirrels and the tedious job of picking out the meat, we never had enough to make it worthwhile.

The other wild crop we picked was persimmons. A persimmon tree is usually not large, about the size of a peach tree. The fruit is about the size of a medium tomato but shaped like an acorn. When the fruit is ripe it is a bright orange color. If picked before they are completely ripe, they have a strong astringent quality, that makes your lips pucker. However, if the persimmons remain on the tree until a good frost, probably into November, they are delicious with a soft sweet interior. They do have lots of seeds. They will ripen at room temperature if picked before they reach their peak. Harvesting the nuts and persimmons made little contribution to our winter food but they were a novelty. We thought it was a case of getting something free—well, almost.

"LeRoy, you'd better get off your school clothes and bring in some wood. Be sure to stack some fireplace wood on the front porch. These nights are getting pretty cool," Mama instructed as I came in the door.

"But I wanted to fly my kite some. The wind's just right," I said pulling off my jacket.

"Get the wood first. If you hurry, maybe you'll still have time."

But the days were getting pretty short and I doubted I would have time that night.

As usual, while I was at school, Daddy had sawed up a huge pile of wood with the engine powered circular saw out near the barn. I first took a load of the small wood in my wagon for the kitchen stove and stacked it in the unfinished room adjoining the kitchen. Next was some larger wood suitable for the furnace in the cellar that heated the living room and took the chill off the other rooms. Finally, two loads of fireplace wood on the front porch and I was done. Not really, I still had the chickens to feed, water and gather the eggs. Sure enough, by the time I had finished these things, the wind had slackened and the sun was setting. No kite flying that night.

We always had a ready supply of wood because about one-third of our farm was wooded. However, it took considerable work to haul the logs from the woods to our woodpile near the barn. We began this job in the fall and continued it throughout the winter whenever the weather permitted. It was always a two-person job.

"I think we'll go to those woods south of the barn and see if we can get a couple wagon loads of logs today. LeRoy, get on your old clothes and I'll hitch up the team to the wagon. Don't forget your gloves,"

Daddy said at breakfast. "I sharpened the crosscut saw a couple days ago so we're ready."

We drove the wagon to the edge of the woods and tied the team to a tree. Mostly we looked for downed trees or dead ones that were standing. Daddy would cut off the small limbs and then we would prepare to saw the trunk of the tree into lengths that we could carry through the woods and load on the wagon. Here's where the crosscut saw came into use and I was going to get some instruction and practice.

"The first thing we need to do is prop up our log somehow so when we make the cut, our saw won't bind. Pull that old stump over here and let's put it right under here where we'll make our first cut," Daddy instructed. "That way the part we cut will fall off and not bind."

When I had wrestled the stump into position under our log, the instruction continued.

"Now, get that crosscut saw over here and you stand on the other side of the log opposite of me. Move in a little closer so it's comfortable to pull the saw a full arm's length. "

We began to saw but at once the saw jammed. Daddy shook his head.

"Don't you remember how we did it last time? Working a crosscut saw is really easy. All you have to remember is— you only pull, never push. If each fellow pulls, the saw never bends or binds. All right, let's try it again," said Daddy.

After a few tries I got the rhythm and we soon had the saw humming its way through the log. Like Daddy said, all I had to remember was just to pull the saw toward me and then let the other fellow pull it back to his side. After we had lugged out of the woods a half dozen logs and loaded them on the wagon, Daddy sat down on a stump and gazed up at the surrounding trees.

"You know, we might as well take down this one; it's dead. I'll show you how to fell it and make it fall just where you want it. Let's drop it over there and it won't hang up in any of these other trees," Daddy said pointing to a small clearing between two large oak trees.

"Now, what we want to do is saw a small wedge out of the side of the tree that faces the direction we want the tree to fall. After we do that, then we'll come around here and make our cut on the opposite side. Get the crosscut saw and you'll see how easy it is. One other thing. When you're sawing, always keep an eye on the tree you're cutting and as soon as it begins to lean, stay clear of it as it falls." Daddy was always careful to point out the dangers of the tasks we did.

We sawed the tree as he had outlined, and it fell just as he had planned right between the two oak trees. I was amazed.

"You see how simple that is," Daddy said, standing back to survey his work. "When you cut the wedge and then saw from the opposite side, it makes a sort of hinge and the tree has to fall just the way you want it."

Learning how to work a crosscut saw and how to safely fell a tree were just a couple of the many tasks Daddy taught me as we went about the daily work on the farm. He was patient in his instructions the first time but he expected me to remember them from that time on. His years of hard work on the farm had taught him how to do every job and he did them with obvious satisfaction. Throughout my life I've used many of the skills he passed on to me.

"Thanksgiving is next week, isn't it?" Daddy asked at the supper table. "I guess the boys will bring up their friends and go hunting as usual."

"Yes, I'm planning a big meal. We have to kill one of those turkeys," Mama answered. "Janice and Thelma both said they would bring something. I told them to make pies; I just don't have time to do that and prepare all the other things for the Thanksgiving meal."

Rabbit hunting season always opened a week before Thanksgiving. It was customary for all my older brothers who were working in Richmond to come up to the farm to hunt on Thanksgiving Day. Furthermore, they would often bring along a friend who wanted to go hunting also. Of course, husbands and boyfriends of my older sisters also joined. Emil was old enough and usually went hunting with the others. I stayed at home and played with Janice's children, Evelyn, Roger and Gretchen. The hunters included my brothers Emil, Robert and Randolph, Janice's husband, Carl, Albert Dassler (friend and coworker of Randolph's), Dick Duvall (another friend of Randolph's) and sometimes Emil Brenckman (the Army Air Corp flyer) would round out the hunting party. With the dogs anxiously running ahead, the hunters headed across the fields and into the woods. At the farmhouse we could hear the excited barking of the dogs when a rabbit was flushed out of his burrow and was quickly followed by one of two shots of a shotgun. As the hunters moved deeper into the woods, the barking of the dogs and an occasional shotgun report grew fainter until we could no longer hear them.

Meanwhile, things were humming in the kitchen. Mama, together with all my sisters and any other wives or girlfriends of my brothers, were preparing the Thanksgiving meal. It would be ready for serving in the late afternoon after the hunters returned. A large fifteen pound turkey was in the oven baking and many hands were busy preparing the other dishes. These included: candied sweet potatoes with marshmallow topping, mashed Irish potatoes, boiled onions with cream sauce, kale, apple and black walnut salad, hot rolls, stuffing, gravy and an assortment of pies. There would be at least two apple pies and two pumpkin ones. Coffee for the adults and milk for the kids. A typical crowd would be about twenty people. It was a feast and all of this company, too. I loved it!

If the weather was good we would play outside. If it was not, there was always that little room over the kitchen which we thought of as our club house. It was always nice and warm there from the register that funneled heat up from the kitchen. You can bet it was plenty warm in that kitchen with that old wood stove going strong and all those people. I know Mama loved having all her children home and working with her in the kitchen. When the last of the food preparation was over, they would all retire to the living room and catch up on all the news of what each one of the children was doing in their work and lives in Richmond. Such talking and laughing you've seldom heard.

There were any number of things we could play outside but one thing was very popular this time of the year—firecrackers. They seemed to come on the market around Thanksgiving and were available until Christmas. We liked the little Chinese firecrackers that were about one and a half inches long and the size of a pencil. They came in packs of twenty-four. One of the things we liked to do was to put them under a tin can with the fuse sticking out. Light the fuse and run away. The pressure buildup would toss the can twenty feet in the air. We were very careful with these firecrackers and none of us ever got injured. I made a little cannon for shooting the firecrackers. The barrel was a short piece of three quarter inch diameter pipe with a screw cap on the back end. The screw-on cap had a hole just big enough for the fuse to poke through. For projectiles we made balls of mud dried in the sun. The firing procedure was to load the firecracker with the fuse sticking out the rear and then push in one of the dried mud balls. The barrel was mounted on a wooden carriage with wheels, just like the real ones. If the mud "cannon ball" was a good fit, a range of twenty to thirty feet was possible. On impact, the mud ball broke apart with a small puff of dust, just the right effect. We made targets on the side of barn and took turns trying to see who was the best shot. Each shot left a spot of brown mud at the point of impact. It was very effective for "war games." I had that cannon for years and never tired of playing with it.

Unless it remained too warm , November was the time of the year for butchering. Ideally, the daytime temperature should not rise above 40 degrees or there was danger of the meat spoiling. We usually butchered a heifer and a hog. Once the animal was dressed out, the carcass was hung up in the smoke house to cure. In the case of beef, a couple days was necessary for the meat to firm and reach its best flavor. Pork normally only took one day to cure. After the curing, the animal was cut up for preserving. Hams and sides of bacon were smoked in the smokehouse; the other cuts were cooked and Mama canned them in glass jars. The traditional jars for canning were Mason Jars. They came in quart and two quart sizes with a wide mouth. The two quart size was well suited for canning some of the larger cuts of meat. First, Mama sterilized the jars by boiling them in hot water. Then the meat was cooked in small enough pieces to go in the jars. Cooking the meat produced a lot of fat which was poured into the jars after the meat had been packed in to seal off the jars. The whole process had to be done very carefully to make sure there was no chance of spoilage. As far as I know, we never had any food poisoning from our preserved meat. Beef patties and sausage were ground up with a hand cranked grinder. Sometimes I got to help in that job. Of course, this was the time of the year when we had plenty of fresh meat to eat—sausage, pork chops, beef patties and other cuts. The beef and pork were canned the same way. It was a period of intense work; Mama was busy in the kitchen cooking and canning and Daddy cut up the meat. The other job I remembered having to do was to keep a good supply of wood available for that wood cook stove in the kitchen. As Mama finished with a batch of meat canned in glass jars, I took them to the cellar and lined them up on the shelves. It was very satisfying to see all the food we had for the coming winter.

Sometimes at Thanksgiving, but always at Christmas, Mama made a mince meat pie. The meat was ground beef with a little suet. After the ground meat was thoroughly cooked in the iron frying pan, apples, raisins, sugar and spices were added to make the pie filling. Mince meat pies were delicious and very special, only available during the holidays.

By the end of November, the days were much shorter and a lot colder. There was ice every morning and occasionally we had some light snow. The trees had shed all their leaves and stood starkly in the woods. The fields surrounding our farmhouse were brown with dried grass and corn stalk stubble. Those lush fields of wheat, corn and our vegetables were only a memory. Quickly, it seemed, winter was upon us.

11

The Car

In 1936 we bought our first car. It was a four-door Chevrolet sedan, gun metal gray. That was a new color in 1936. Auto colors prior to that were mostly black with some maroon, a few forest greens and fewer still dark blue. The price was $700 from the Luck Motor Company in Ashland. None of us living at home at that time, Mama, Daddy, Emil or I, had ever driven a car. I was eleven and Emil was fifteen. In Virginia you could get a license to drive on the highways only, not in any city, at age twelve, provided an adult was with you in the car. Funny thing, the adult did not have to be a driver. Having a car gave us a degree of freedom we had never before experienced. Before the car, we were limited to either horseback or driving the farm wagon. Of course, we had ridden in the cars of other members of our family when they had visited the farm from Richmond.

Driving instruction was normally provided by the salesman who sold you the car. So we had an instructor, but who was to learn to drive? Daddy had no interest. Mama, then fifty-four years old, took a couple lessons but couldn't manage the clutch, gear shift, steering, brake and gas pedal all together. She became very agitated and soon gave up the whole thing. In earlier years she had driven a team of horses pulling a wagon or other farm equipment with no problems. This new fangled automobile was too much for her. She said someone else would have to drive. Funny that this was never a consideration before we bought the car. Probably she thought she could manage it. There weren't many things Mama couldn't do if she put her mind to it, unfortunately, driving the car was one of them. Well, that boiled down the choices to Emil as the likely prospective driver. Emil caught on quickly and soon was able to get his beginner's license in Ashland and so became the designated family driver. I know Mama badly wanted to have a car to give her some freedom to leave the farm and visit friends in and around Doswell and to go to St. Martin's Church in Doswell. In addition, I am sure she wanted to visit her brothers and sisters in Richmond and members of our family who lived there.

At the time I was too young even to be allowed to take driving instruction much less to get a permit. Like most boys of my age I was fascinated by all mechanical things. I got Daddy to help me make a sort of driving simulator from old odds and ends we found in the barn. First, on a two foot pine board, we mounted three large bolts with a spring under the head of each bolt. These were parts off of an old piece of junk farm machinery. These would serve as the clutch, brake and gas pedal along with a little imagination. Each of the pedals had a strong spring so I could get the feel of coordinating the clutch and gas. The gear shift was a piece of iron rod which I stuck into the ground to my right. I made cuts in the lawn in the form of an "H" (the gearshift pattern for the standard three speed and reverse.) The steering wheel was a baby buggy wheel with the axle stuck in the ground. All this was set up in the yard under the shade of one of those big black walnut trees. Mama allowed me to bring outside an old straight chair; this completed my "driver's position." I spent many hours "driving" and fantasizing in my stationary car. Sometimes I was driving one of the big trucks I saw on the highway on my way to school; other times I imagined I was driving Mama to church. This crude "car simulator" gave me enough feel for the mechanics of driving so that a year later at the age of twelve, I got my beginner's license. Of course, Emil let me practice some on our real car before I went to take the test.

We had only had the car a few months when Mama suggested one

Sunday that we drive down to Richmond to visit my sister Janice and her family. We could also see Mama's sister, Hettie, and her brother, Page. Janice lived on the same property as Aunt Hettie and Uncle Page. Emil was the only one with a license so he drove. We had a nice visit and decided in the afternoon we had better start home. There was a light rain falling and dark clouds promised more of the same. Even starting in mid-afternoon it would be nearly dark when we reached the farm. There were the usual farm chores to do before dark: milking the cows, feeding the horses and cows, bringing in the sheep and collecting the eggs from the hen houses, to name a few.

The light rain continued as we said our good-byes and started out. Daddy rode in the front with Emil; Mama and I were in the back. Only a couple miles from Janice's we turned onto Williamsburg Road. It was a wide street with a number of turns and headed downhill. As we rounded a left-handed turn, I saw a car coming fast at us. Mama yelled out, "He's gonna hit us!"

The oncoming car was coming too fast to make the turn and was headed for our left front fender. Seconds later the car smashed head-on into us, hitting the front left side, the driver's side. The impact threw Emil against the steering wheel and the windshield; Daddy smashed into the windshield on the passenger side; Mama was thrown forward against the back of the front seat and I found myself on the floor between the front and back seats. I was dazed with bruises but nothing more. Emil was knocked unconscious and slumped over the twisted steering wheel. Daddy had blood on his head and was clearly dazed, but managed to get out of the car. Mama was clearly hurt and kept holding her chest and moaning. I was so frightened. I was afraid Emil had been killed. I knew I should get him out of the car as fast as possible because it might catch on fire. The driver's side was completely smashed. The only way was to drag him out the passenger side. The gear shift was on the floor for this car—right in the way to dragging Emil out.

There was no one to help me. Daddy was dazed and sitting on the ground holding his head and Mama was nearby crying in pain and calling for me to hurry and get Emil out. I was panicked. After several tries I managed to pull Emil over the gearshift and out of the car onto the ground. He was completely unconscious. By then someone had called an ambulance and both Emil and Daddy were taken to a hospital. Mama wanted to return to her sister Hettie's house and I went there with her.

Emil had a concussion and stayed in the hospital for several days. Daddy had head and chest injuries but was released in two days to return to the farm. After Mama was examined by a doctor, it was determined that she had two broken ribs and severe bruises. I was the only one who had no injuries, just some bruises. Mama and I stayed a week at Aunt Hettie's. For me it was a holiday because I could play with Roger, Gretchen and Evelyn, Janice's children, who lived next door. Despite the lack of any serious physical injuries, I had nightmares of that accident for a long time. First there was the awful crash and then my struggle of trying to get Emil out of the wrecked car. Many nights I cried out and woke up in a sweat, reliving that head-on crash. The driver of the other car had been speeding and, to make matters worse, he left the scene of the accident. A long legal battle ensued, but in the end the hospital bills were covered and we got money to buy a new 1937 Chevrolet sedan. Same color, gun metal gray, same four-door sedan, just a year newer.

One Sunday summer morning, Emil and I asked Mama if we could take the car and drive out to Doswell and get some gas and maybe stop and talk to the Carter boys. This was not a Sunday when there was a service at St. Martin's Church in Doswell so Mama agreed. We drove out to Doswell and up to the gas station on the highway. When we had gassed up, Emil said, " Let's take a little drive on some of the back roads. I don't want to visit your friends—the Carters."

Well, I was a little disappointed but I was enjoying the freedom of riding in the car so I agreed. We had gone out of Doswell only a few miles when we passed a field full of watermelons.

"Those watermelons ought to be ripe," said Emil, braking the car to a stop on the shoulder of the road.

"What are you doing?" I asked.

"Look, there's a whole field of them and there's nobody around on a Sunday morning." Emil was pointing to the watermelons. "You hop out and get one of those close to the road. I'll pull over a little farther and get off the road. OK?"

The road had quite a crown and there was a small ditch on the right. The ground sloped up sharply beyond the ditch to the level of the watermelon field beyond. Emil maneuvered the car over on the shoulder and close to the ditch. "Just hop out and leave the door open so you can get in quick when you come back with that melon. Hurry."

I had visions of a farmer appearing over that hill with his shotgun as I swung out of the car leaving the door open. I grabbed the first watermelon at the edge of the field and ran back to the car. I got into the front seat holding the watermelon in my lap. Before I had time to get the door closed, Emil said, "OK, let's get out of here."

He backed the car just a little and all at once I realized the door was jammed against that bank.

"Stop!" I yelled. But it was too late. There was a sharp snap of metal breaking and the door fell off into the ditch. It was at that instant that Emil realized what had happened.

"What the hell? You broke the door off! Now what are we going to do?" He was getting mad.

"You didn't give me time to close the door. It's not my fault," I said.

Well, the damage was done. The door had jammed into the bank and when Emil backed the car the hinges were snapped off. We picked up the door, wiped off as much mud as we could and Emil put it into place.

"Now you are gonna have to hold the door while I drive. For God's sake, don't let it go. We've gotta figure out how to get this thing home and then get it repaired without Mama and Daddy knowing about it."

We were a couple of scared kids. Taking the watermelon was bad enough, but breaking off the car door was real trouble!

Lucky for us the car garage was out beyond the garden not far from the barn. We drove in with me holding that door for dear life and casually returned to the house. We hid the watermelon in the straw stack behind the barn. We told Mama and Daddy nothing of our morning escapade. We made up a story about a baseball game to be held in Doswell on the next morning and got permission to use the car again. We had to get that door repaired before our parents found out. We pooled all our savings from the vegetables and fruits we had sold to the people around Doswell in the past weeks. Our plan was set; we would leave early Monday morning and pretending to go to that baseball game we would go instead to Richmond and try to get the door repaired. Fortunately we found an auto repair place on the outskirts of Richmond and a man who said he could replace the hinges in an hour or so. He gave us an estimate and it pretty much cleaned us out of our "vegetable" savings. We were plenty anxious waiting for the repair to be done and to get back to Doswell. When the work was done, we paid up and drove back to Doswell. Hardly a word was spoken. We knew we had done a bad thing—really two bad things—and we were ashamed of ourselves. Too ashamed to admit it to our parents—ever. Neither of us ever told our parents about the "Sunday watermelon escapade."

With our car we now could occasionally drive the seven miles down to Ashland where they had a movie theater. Mama and Daddy especially liked the movies starring Will Rogers; I enjoyed them myself. One of my favorites was "Steamboat Round the Bend" with Will Rogers and Marie Dressler. There were a lot of movies in the mid-30's. Errol Flynn was popular in several pirate movies. And then there were the ever-popular westerns with stars like John Wayne and Roy Rogers. John Wayne made "Westward Ho" and "King of the Pecos" in 1935 when I was ten. Shirley Temple was about my age and I really liked her movies. I remember "Little Colonel" with Lionel Barrymore and "Littlest Rebel" where she danced with the famous tap dancer, Bill Robinson. In these years, movies were a great diversion from the hard times of the Depression.

In January 1937 I was twelve and proceeded at once to get my driving license. I was restricted, of course, to rural travel and needed an adult to accompany me. It was a strange law that did not require the adult to be a driver, but I suppose the adult was intended to ensure that the young driver did not engage in dangerous driving habits. Once I had my driver's license it meant a great step in freedom for us. By that time, Emil had moved to Richmond to finish his high school education so I became the family driver. I was tall for my age, but at twelve years old I still couldn't see over the steering wheel or the dash when I sat in our Chevrolet. So I always sat on a big pillow when I drove to give me a good view over the dashboard. Often when Mama and I drove out on US Highway #1, we would be pulled over by the State Police. It happened once when we were on our way to Ashland. We had crossed the South Anna River where the Ashland Flour Mill was and were going up that long grade. Near the top of the grade I heard a siren. A quick glance in the rear view mirror revealed a police car following us.

"Is that a police siren?" Mama asked, looking over at me.

"Yep, it sure is and he's following us. I know I was only doing fifty-five."

"You'd better pull over," Mama cautioned.

I slowed and once we topped the grade I eased the car onto the shoulder and came to a stop. I couldn't imagine what I was doing wrong. I rolled down the window and waited nervously while the policeman walked up to our car. He was a Virginia State policeman, the ones who wore those campaign hats with the broad brim. He bent and looked in the window at me and across at Mama.

"How old are you, Sonny? Good morning, ma'am."

"Twelve," I answered, nervously.

"How long've you been driving?"

"He's a good driver, Officer; he's very careful. I'm sure he wasn't speeding." Mama jumped to my defense before I could answer.

"Since my twelfth birthday," I answered.

"And when might that have been?" The policeman was getting a little frustrated.

"The second of January of this year," I added, like I was revealing a big secret.

"So, that would make about seven months, wouldn't it? Let me see your driving permit." Now the policeman was getting down to the important things. Mama opened the glove compartment, retrieved my permit and handed it across to the policeman. He studied it a minute and passed it back to me.

"Well, Sonny, you seem to be doing just fine. I stopped you because you looked awfully young. While we're stopped, how about if I just ask you a couple questions about driving."

I was imagining a test on those traffic rules that I had taken when I got my permit. I began to perspire and waited for the first question.

"What's the speed limit out here on this highway?"

"Fifty-five," I answered confidently.

"O.K., suppose you come up to a railroad crossing, what should you do?" Now the policeman's questions were ranging farther.

"I would stop before I got on the tracks and look both ways before I drove across," I offered.

"O.K., now show me the hand signals."

"Well, if I put my left arm out and hold it down like this, it means I'm going to slow down or stop. For a left turn signal, I stick my arm straight out. And for a right turn, I put my arm up like this." I knew I was right on this one.

"O.K., Sonny, drive carefully. Good day, ma'am." The policeman gave me a pat on the shoulder and headed back to his car. I looked across at Mama and she was smiling.

"Wasn't he a nice man. Now let's drive on," Mama said.

Occurrences like this were pretty common. I was comfortable driving on the highways and the back roads, but the traffic, such as we encountered in the town of Ashland, was a little nerve wracking. I guess I did look pretty young perched up on my pillow driving that big Chevrolet sedan. After all, there weren't that many twelve year olds out driving on a busy highway like US #1.

Daddy seldom went with us, but Mama and I made numerous short trips in the car. I know she felt she had been confined to the farm for too many years. One of her friends, Miss Deanie Hunter, lived about five miles away across the North Anna River on the road to Hanover Courthouse. Miss Deanie, as we called her, had two sons about my age. Sometimes Mama and I would drive over and I would play ball with the boys in a meadow below the house while Mama visited. Miss Deanie always had cold lemonade and cookies for us when we came up to her house after playing. She served tea and little sweets to Mama using a beautiful china teapot with matching cups. It seemed quite a formal affair from our informal meals on the farm. I know Mama enjoyed the change. There was a certain formality and mystery surrounding Miss Deanie which always fascinated me. She always wore a black glove on her left hand and never seemed to use that hand much. Whether her hand was deformed or had a missing finger, I never knew. Mama reminded me it was impolite to stare and cautioned me never to ask about that mysterious hand in the black glove. The other thing I wondered, why was she called "Miss Deanie" and yet she had two boys. Were they hers? Had she ever been married? These questions were never answered but I always liked to go there. I know Mama enjoyed visiting her and so we often did.

With our new mobility, Mama and I began to attend the little church in Doswell, St. Martin's Episcopal Church. Mama had been brought up in St. John's Episcopal Church in Richmond and felt comfortable in this one. Daddy's family in Maryland was Methodist, but he took no interest in church and never went with us. The church in Doswell was small and rather plain, but it still had a certain charm. It had white siding with a black shingle roof topped by a traditional steeple. Church service was only held once a month when a "traveling clergy" visited it. It was too small to support a full time rector. I liked the pageantry of the Episcopal service with the candles, acolytes, the colorful robes of the clergy and the altar hangings which changed in color with the seasons of the Church year. At first, the "getting ups and kneeling downs" of the Episcopalians, as some characterized their actions during the service, were confusing to me. They stood and prayed sometimes; other times they knelt. When they sang the hymns, they always stood. Their responses came from *The Book of Common Prayer*. Every pew had *The Book of Common Prayer* along with the *Hymnal*. I soon began to appreciate the "ups and downs"; they made those straight-backed wooded pews tolerable. I was not yet confirmed but I went up to the communion rail with Mama and crossed my arms across my chest for a blessing instead of receiving the bread and wine.

Just before we left our pew to go up for the communion, the congregation always said a prayer which contained this statement: *We are not worthy so much as to gather up the crumbs under thy Table.* Often when I was kneeling at the communion rail with Mama, my eyes would drift down to the area around the base of the altar table to see if there were any crumbs. Soon these childish wool-gatherings disappeared and I began to appreciate the service. Attendance at this little Episcopal church began a habit of worship that I continued all my life.

Before we had a car, Emil and I used to take the farm wagon every Saturday and load it with fresh summer vegetables and fruits and go to Doswell to sell them door to door. In July and August we would have sweet corn, string beans, butter beans, tomatoes, squash, summer apples, red cherries, strawberries, watermelons, cantaloupes, peaches and other things depending on our garden and fruit trees. We developed regular customers who looked for us every Saturday. This was a source of money not available in other times of the year. Of course, we only kept a small portion of the money earned; most of it went to Mama for family necessities. Later, when we had our car and I was driving, Mama and I continued this source of income, but now we expanded our territory to Richmond. During the summer we loaded the car with all the fresh vegetables and fruit we could haul and drove the twenty miles down to Richmond. I was still not qualified to drive in the city, so we were careful to park the car in a nice neighborhood just outside the northern city limits. Then we canvassed the homes. By noon or early afternoon we had sold out. Mama's nephew, Richmond Price, and his wife lived in this neighborhood. Occasionally we would stop for a visit before returning to the farm. Those experiences of selling fruits and vegetables from our car taught me a lot about money and how to approach people if you wanted to sell something.

12

Biplanes and Biscuits

The plane roared directly over our farmhouse not more than about three hundred feet high. It was olive drab color with stars under each wing and red, white and blue stripes on the tail. It was a biplane that reminded me of the pictures of those World War I airplanes I had seen in the "Saturday Evening Post." When the biplane was over the northern edge of our farm, it banked sharply to the left and began a circle back toward our barn. I was so excited as I watched it.

I ran from the yard and yelled through the kitchen screen door, "Mama, Mama, that plane is going to land! He's circling right now!"

Mama had heard the plane's roar, too, and she quickly came outside drying her hands on her apron. The plane had completed its circle and passed over our barn as Mama took my hand and we hurried out of the yard where we could see better. This time the plane was even lower, and not flying so fast. I just knew it was going to land. It completed another circle and went south away from our farmhouse.

"I guess he's not going to land after all," Mama told me.

But just then we saw it coming back low over the trees and headed for the pasture below our barn.

"Mama, Mama, he did come back! I know he's going to land in our pasture!" I said excitedly, squeezing Mama's hand.

The biplane slipped low over the trees and touched down in the pasture. It bounced across the rough pasture with the tail high and turned sharply just before it got to the fence on the far side. Then the pilot revved up the engine and taxied back toward our end of the pasture. Mama and I stood on the hill near our barn, which overlooked the pasture, and we could see everything. By that time Daddy had also heard and seen the plane from the field where he had been repairing a fence. He walked down toward the pasture as the plane taxied back. My brother, Emil, came out from behind the barn and also headed down toward the pasture, running. I don't know where he had been unless he had been helping Daddy with that fence. Well, my brother just raced for the pasture fence and climbed over fast like he was afraid the plane might leave before he could get there. There were two pilots and they got out and my Daddy shook hands with them. They walked across the pasture and up the hill by the barn toward Mama and me.

As they came closer, Mama exclaimed, "Why it's Emil Brenckman!"

"Hello, Mrs. Day", said Emil with a twinkle in his eye. "Bet you didn't expect me, did you?" Then he broke out in a broad smile and laughed as he gave Mama a firm hug.

My brother, Emil, was named after Emil Brenckman, so it always got a little confusing when the two were together. Of course, this seldom happened. Emil Brenckman introduced the other pilot and we all walked toward the farmhouse. My brother and I tagged along behind dividing our attention between looking at these two real aviators and an occasional glance back at the biplane in the pasture. I think we were so excited it was hard to convince ourselves that this was really happening.

Emil Brenckman was a good friend of our family and he was in the Army Air Corp. The Brenckmans and the Pflugradts had lived years ago on Bullfield, the farm next to us. In fact, that's how my oldest sister, Janice, had met and married her husband, Carl Pflugradt. Both families had come to this country just before World War I. Naturally we were good friends with all of the Brenckmans and the Pflugradts having lived close to them for years. They had moved away from Bullfield before I was born. Emil Brenckman was the same age as my older sisters and brothers and Mama and Daddy treated him like a son. He was always the happy one and full of good stories and jokes. He was also famous for his pranks.

When we reached the shade of our yard, Mama invited Emil and his fellow pilot to sit and explain how they happened to land at our farm. At first, Mama was concerned that there was some problem with the plane and that's why they had landed.

Taking off his helmet and goggles, Emil laughed and explained, "No, Mrs. Day. Everything is fine just as I explained to Mr. Day down in the field. We were on a training hop out of Langley Field and I just told my friend here that it would be fun to fly up here and surprise you. So we did."

As the conversation continued, I stood by Mama's chair and looked at every detail of the flying uniforms worn by Emil Brenckman and his fellow pilot. Besides the customary helmet and goggles, they each wore a leather flight jacket, jodhpur trousers and shiny leather boots. I was mesmerized being this close to real "flying aviators." I had seen pictures of them with their white scarves, helmets and goggles—but here they were—right in my own yard.

"You will stay for lunch, won't you? I just made some cold tea and we're having hot biscuits with our lunch," Mama said.

"No thanks. We can't stay long or they'll miss us at the base and then we'll be in real trouble. Thanks anyway," Emil replied.

But Mama insisted and wasn't going to let this "aviator visitor" leave without something to eat. "Well, I'll just bring out some nice cold tea from the spring house and some of the biscuits I just baked. At least you can have that much before you fly back to Langley Field. It'll only take me a minute".

Mama hurriedly left for the house and my brother and I stayed while Daddy talked to the two pilots. I could hardly believe this was happening. Imagine, a real airplane landing right here in our pasture!

Emil Brenckman and his fellow pilot enjoyed the cold tea and the biscuits with fresh made butter. They ate quickly and then said they needed to get airborne and return to Langley Field. They said goodbye and Daddy and my brother walked with them down to the plane.

I stayed close to Mama as we watched from the hill near our barn. Daddy and Emil Brenckman lifted the tail and the other pilot pushed on the propeller and moved the plane as far back as they could against the fence. That would give them the maximum takeoff distance. On takeoff they had to clear that fence on the far side of the pasture. Emil Brenckman climbed into the rear cockpit and the other pilot prepared to swing the prop to start the plane.

"Switch off." I heard the Emil Brenckman call out to the other pilot who stood ready to swing the prop.

After a couple pull throughs of the prop, Emil called out, " Switch on." Then the pilot swung the prop as hard as he could but the engine did not fire.

"Why don't they just start the engine?" I asked Mama.

"Well, that's what they're trying to do. I certainly hope Emil was right when he said they didn't have any problem." Mama was becoming a little concerned, too.

Again we heard a call from the cockpit, "Switch off." This was followed by a few more slow pull throughs of the prop. Next was the call, "Switch on." Now the man at the front of the airplane gave a vigorous pull on the prop which produced a cough of the engine and a lot of smoke out of the exhaust. Still the engine refused to run. The whole procedure was repeated once more and this time the engine gave a cough followed by a loud sputtering of the engine. The pilot ran back to his cockpit and climbed in while Emil Brenckman warmed up the engine.

"They're goin', Mama! They're gonna takeoff now, aren't they?" I stamped my foot in excitement and tugged on her hand.

"Yes. It looks like they've got the plane running all right. I certainly hope they can take off before they get to that fence." Mama was a little worried.

What a racket the engine made when the pilot advanced the throttle and the plane began to roll! I saw Emil Brenckman give a wave from the rear cockpit and the plane quickly began to pick up speed. I was fascinated watching the takeoff. Then I saw the tail was up and quickly the plane lifted from the pasture and was over the fence and climbing. They climbed straight ahead and almost disappeared from sight when

I saw him bank to the left and return toward the farmhouse. We waved and I could see both pilots waving as they passed overhead. The plane headed south away from the farm and was out of sight in a minute. Never had I experienced anything like that visit of Emil Brenckman in the biplane that landed in our pasture.

Weeks after the biplane incident I used to go down to the pasture and look at the scarred turf where the tail skid had dug up the grass when the pilot had spun the plane around for takeoff. I replayed the whole experience in my mind over and over so I would never forget even one detail. This event happened when I was six years old and not yet in school. My brother, Emil, and I were the only ones there except for Mama and Daddy. I don't know how my brother happened to be home. My older brothers and sisters were either in school or, in the case of the oldest ones, had already left the farm. So my brother, Emil, and I, along with Mama and Daddy, were the only witnesses of this exciting time. I was not yet in school because I had had pneumonia and whooping cough that winter and Mama kept me home and taught me the basics of the first grade. I started in the second grade the next year.

Our farm was more or less on a line from Richmond to Washington and we saw lots of airplanes fly over. One day we saw a dirigible come right over our house. It was huge and traveled so slowly that it took several minutes to pass. It was low enough that we could clearly see the engine pods and the gondola. The dirigible was painted silver and was some sight to see. It may have been either the Shenadoah or the Macon which were very much in the news at that time. This was a time of great interest in aviation. Only four years earlier, Lindbergh had made his famous solo flight across the Atlantic in 1927. He was very much in the news with his other pioneering flights looking for routes PanAm could use on flights to the Orient and South America.

*Emil Brenckman, the pilot who landed his
Army biplane on our farm. Circa 1930.*

Emil Brenckman proudly shows off his Model T Ford.

Despite the Depression, the 30's were a time of great innovation and exploration in the field of aviation. It is often referred to as the "

Golden Age" of aviation. In 1932 Amelia Earhart was the first woman to fly solo across the Atlantic. She flew from Newfoundland to Ireland. I followed all these events with great interest although I was just a youngster. These aviation pioneers were my heroes. Admiral Richard Byrd's flight in Antartica, Howard Hughes flight around the world in 1938, Wiley Post and Will Rogers' flight and tragic crash—all of these sparked my interest in airplanes. There were also speed records across the country, altitude records, the Cleveland Air Races and the Thompson Trophy Races and barnstorming. At an early age my interest in airplanes turned to building model airplanes. My first ones were rather crude solid scale models carved from soft white pine wood. I played with these models letting my imagination take me on trips to far away places or dog fighting in imaginary air battles. Later when I was about ten, I began to build rubber powered flying models of balsa and tissue. I had a Wakefield with a wingspan of about twenty-four inches that was a great flyer. We had plenty of open space out near the barn and it was a good place to fly my model airplanes. At about this age I read everything I could find that had anything to do with airplanes. The magazine, "Popular Mechanics", always had stories of futuristic airplanes that interested me. Sometimes "Popular Mechanics" had articles on how to build your own airplane. I could only dream about such a possibility. Looking back, I guess my lifelong love of airplanes began that spring morning when Emil Brenckman's biplane landed in our pasture.

13

Farm Traumas

Daddy's Fall

I was upstairs in my bedroom alcove playing with one of my airplanes when I heard Mama call out excitedly, "LeRoy, come quickly! Your Daddy's been hurt bad!"

Her frantic call scared me and I hurried down the stairs and into the kitchen. As I ran in the kitchen, Daddy was slumped in a chair with his back to me and Mama was bending over him. When she looked up, I could see the panic in her face. Then I noticed a big bath towel wrapped around Daddy's neck and it was all covered with blood.

"What happened to Daddy?"

"He fell through the upper floor in the barn and onto the hay mower below," Mama replied, wrapping another towel about Daddy's neck. "He's got a cut on his neck and I can't stop the bleeding."

The first towel was soaked red with blood. I hadn't seen that much blood since we butchered the calf last fall. My throat choked up but I managed to get out, "Mama, is he going to die?"

"No, of course not. But he's losing a lot of blood. You're going to have to ride over to the Cannons and tell them to get Dr. Wright. You can saddle up the horse, can't you?" Mama was calming down now and trying not to scare me any more than necessary. "LeRoy, you've got to hurry. Do you understand?"

"Yes, Mama. I'll saddle up Billy right now." I tried to sound like this was no big deal, but my voice was squeaky and my legs felt rubbery. I had put the saddle on our horse once before with Daddy supervising, but this time I was on my own.

"You know that someone at the Cannons will have to go out to Doswell in order to telephone Dr. Wright. So be sure to tell them how bad Daddy is hurt and they must not waste any time. Do you understand, LeRoy?" Mama was trying to convey the urgency of the situation to a twelve-year old without panicking me.

"Yes, Mama. I'm going right now." As I squeezed around Daddy's chair to go out the kitchen door, I looked back at him and saw the second towel was now getting soaked with blood. His usual ruddy complexion was a pasty white. My throat tightened again and I hurried out the kitchen door and ran to the barn.

I had never seen this much blood on anyone before. Not even the terrible car accident that happened the year before was anything like this. I was afraid that Daddy was going to die. But right now I had to focus on getting the horse, Billy, saddled up. It was just dusk and getting a little dark inside the barn when I got to Billy's stall. I started to open the stall and suddenly I had a terrible need to see where Daddy had fallen on the mower. The mower was the type that had a long arm with a blade that moved back and forth as the mower was pulled by the two horses. The blade arm consisted of a series of individual trapezoidal blades. I knew how sharp those individual blades were; I had seen Daddy filing them many times. When the mower was parked in the barn, the long arm with the cutting blade was raised to a near vertical position so the machine didn't take up so much room. Even in the poor light I could see blood on the blade and on the dirt floor below the mower. I looked up and saw where the flooring on the second level had broken through allowing Daddy to fall. We knew there were places in the upper floor that were rotten and needed replacing, but like so many things we just hadn't gotten around to them. Probably Daddy had gone up there to throw down some hay for the horses and cows. We also kept some of the wheat up there; maybe he was after some of that for chicken feed.

I didn't have time to worry about that now; I had to get Billy saddled up and hurry to the next farm and tell the Cannons. I put the bridle on Billy before I got him out of the stall and then brought him out and tied him to one of the posts in the center of the barn. I had saddled him up only a couple times so I was desperately trying to remember the routine. First, throw the saddle blanket over his back. Then I got the saddle from the rack and hoisted it up on him. Billy gave a shudder as if to say, "Hey, Boy. What are you up to this time of the night?" I gave him a reassuring pat on the rump and started to adjust the saddle. Now where's that belly band? Of course, it's just hanging on the far side of the horse. I reached under the horse's belly, grabbed the belly band and hooked it up. "Always be sure you cinch it up good or you'll just pull the saddle over on you when you try to mount the horse," Daddy had said when he was checking me out on the process of saddling up one day. I cinched up the belly band tight, pulled on the saddle horn to ensure the saddle was stable and hurriedly untied Billy and led him out of the barn. All of this had only taken a few minutes but Mama's words about hurrying and that sight of Daddy with all the blood on the towel around his neck flashed through my mind. I grabbed the saddle horn, strained to reach my left foot high enough to get into the stirrup and gave a tug hoping to swing up into the saddle. But Billy had other ideas. He made a couple sideways steps away from me just as I tried to swing up into the saddle. I didn't make it and found myself with my left foot in the stirrup, hopping on my right trying to get into position for another try.

"Whoa, Billy. Good boy. Whoa, now."

Billy was actually the gentlest of our horses and I felt pretty safe with him. Another try and I made it up into the saddle and we were off around the barn and into the road down the hill to the flats and headed for the Cannon farm. It was about a mile from our house to the Cannons' house.

I don't know where or why Daddy bought the horse, Billy. He was certainly not a work horse, not what we called a "plow horse."

We already had two work animals: Molly, our dependable mule, and Albert, a younger horse with a club foot. Daddy said he damaged his foot when it got caught in a wire fence when he was just a colt. Anyway, both were good work animals. But Billy was different. He was more refined. He always seemed to resent it when he had to pull a plow or team up with one of the others to pull the hay wagon. He was better mannered; seldom ever gave an angry kick or acted stubborn when it was time to pull. But the best thing about Billy was he had the most relaxing canter of any horse I had ever ridden. He could break into a gallop that was just a rolling motion like being in a rocking chair—well almost. And he didn't have to be going at breakneck speed either. It was a joy to ride him. Of course, you weren't supposed to ride farm horses. And I never did ride Albert or Molly except when they were hitched up to a wagon or when Daddy had me ride Molly when he was cultivating our garden. That was because the rows were pretty close together and extra care was necessary to keep from plowing up the tomatoes, squash or whatever. Daddy would concentrate or guiding the cultivator, depending on me to keep the horse or mule straight down the row and out of the vegetables.

I kept Billy at a steady gallop as we crossed the flats and turned onto the road that led up to the Cannon's place. Their farm had been called Bullfield for generations. It had once belonged to Mr. Doswell who sold our farm, Hilldene, to Mama and Daddy. I slowed Billy to a walk as we crossed the small wooden bridge over the creek and headed up the hill to their house. Billy was sweating heavily by now and I was out of breath from the ride and the anxiety. I rode right up into their yard; they didn't have any fence around it like we did. I tried to yell out but my mouth was dry and I could only make a garbled sound.

Finally, I got it out, "Hello. Hello. Anybody home! Help! My Daddy's been hurt! Manley, Leonard, Mozelle, anybody!!"

"Who's there? Hey, boy. Oh, it's the Day boy. Come for help. What's the matter?" Manley came down the steps carrying a kerosene lantern, and shielding his eyes with one hand trying to see me.

"My Daddy's been cut something awful! He fell through the barn floor and hit the mower. Mama's taking care of him now but if we don't get a doctor—-he's bleeding awful. Mama says you gotta go to Doswell and phone for Dr. Wright. You can, can't you? You gotta!" My words were spilling out between sobs.

"Now, Boy. Things gonna be all right. I'll get the horse saddled up real quick and head for Doswell and call Dr. Wright. You just head on back home and tell your mama that everything's gonna be all right. You done real good coming over here. You being just a young-un. Now you get on home and best you let that horse take it easy. He looks mighty sweated up."

Dr. Wright lived just a mile or so outside of the town of Doswell. He was the only doctor in our area. People just took care of their ailments as best as they could, only calling on Dr. Wright for a real serious illness and accidents. It was well past supper time before Mama and I heard his Model A Ford coming in our road. Mama had earlier put another bandage around Daddy's neck and he was resting quietly in his bed. He had lost a lot of blood and was weak but at least Mama had finally stopped the terrible bleeding. Mama got up from her chair and went to the door to meet Dr. Wright. She stepped outside to talk to him. I guess she didn't want me to hear how badly Daddy was hurt. Pretty soon Dr. Wright stepped into the room and went directly to the bedroom to see Daddy. Mama came out and took in a basin of hot water and some clean cloths. Dr. Wright and Mama were in there a long time and I just waited outside. I was afraid to hear what the doctor would say about Daddy. Finally Dr. Wright and Mama came out and went into the kitchen. He spent a long time washing his hands and talked so softly with Mama that I couldn't hear.

When he came into the living room where I was, he said, "Well, young man. Your mother has told me how brave you were to ride over to the neighbors and get them to call me. You did a good thing. Your daddy's going to be all right. He's lost a lot of blood but he'll be all right after a few days. Guess you'll have to be the man of the family and help out your mother. Goodnight, Mrs. Day. If Mr. Day has any more bleeding or other problems, just get someone to give me a call."

Don't Race That Horse

Nearly every Sunday one or more of my older brothers and/or sisters would drive up from Richmond to visit and have Sunday supper with us. Supper was the evening meal; dinner was the midday meal. They would usually bring along their current boyfriend/girlfriend or spouse if they were married. It was an inexpensive outing for them and good entertainment for those of us stuck on the farm. I always looked forward to the Sundays when we expected some company. These were the days before we had a car so Mama didn't get to go to church. That meant she would start in the morning to get some of the cooking done before the company came. Both Mama and Daddy enjoyed having their children visit although it meant some extra work. In the summertime, supper might be fried chicken, corn on the cob, string beans or lima beans, Irish potatoes and hot biscuits. We children picked the beans and corn from the garden on Saturday and had them ready for cooking on Sunday. Daddy was up early on Sunday morning to milk the cows and put them out to pasture along with the horses. I did my chores with the chickens. Mama was busy in the kitchen preparing some of the food with some reluctant help from my sister, Margaret. Margaret, the remaining girl on the farm, was in high school and looking forward to the day when she would graduate and could leave the farm. Each of my brothers and sisters had done that as soon as they finished school.

If fried chicken was on the menu, that meant Daddy had to kill several of the chickens and we had to pluck the feathers before they were taken in to Mama for dressing and cooking. The chickens we ate were the young pullets, not the laying hens. Often I would go with Daddy to the chicken pen and help him catch the ones we were going to kill. I held them by their legs while Daddy would take one and chop off its head on a big stump near the hen house. I always hated this part of the job. Not because I had any particular love for the chickens, quite the contrary, but all that blood—-! Earlier Daddy had built a fire under a big cast iron pot in the back of the house. When that water was hot, nearly boiling, we would hold the dead chicken by its legs and douse it in the water for a minute. Then came the tedious job of plucking off all the feathers. Not only all the regular feathers, but we had to get all those little hairy ones, too. If that chicken wasn't completely clean and naked, Mama would send it back outside for some more plucking. It was not a job I enjoyed but thinking about that delicious fried chicken for supper made it tolerable.

If it was early in the summer, we had strawberries. By late July or August the peaches would be ripe. We had six peach trees on the side of the hill just below the farmhouse. Any of that fruit would make delicious ice cream. For this weekend Mama decided we should have peach ice cream. That meant someone had to go out to Campbell's Store in Doswell on Saturday and get a block of ice.

When I brought the string beans into the kitchen that I had picked in the garden, Mama said, "LeRoy, tell your Daddy to hitch up the horse and you go out to Doswell and get fifty pounds of ice. Tomorrow we'll make some ice cream when all the folks are here. Would you like that?"

"Sure, Mama. Who's coming?"

"Well, the letter from Janice said they would be up. Maybe some of the others," Mama replied as she busied about the kitchen.

"Then Gretchen, Roger and Evelyn will be coming, too."

"Of course, LeRoy. Don't they always bring their children. Don't be silly. Go and tell your father to hitch up the horse and come back and I'll give you some money for the ice."

"Mama says I have to go to Doswell for some ice. We're having ice cream tomorrow. Will you hitch up Billy to the jumper?"

I found Daddy in the barn putting some straw in one of the stalls. He put down his pitchfork and he and I rolled the jumper around to the back door of the barn. We called this one-horse vehicle a "jumper." It was related to the racing sulky, I suppose. It had two high wheels, a high seat just wide enough for two people to squeeze into and a sort of basket made of oak staves for your feet and whatever else you were carrying. It was light and easy for a horse to pull. It was the best thing to use if you could carry all your load in that sort of basket at your feet.

"Now here's the money for the ice. Get fifty pounds because it's awfully hot and a lot of it's going to melt before Sunday. Do you have some burlap bags to wrap around the ice to keep it from melting?"

Mama's instructions were always very specific, always covering all details. She thought of everything. I learned a lot from the way she thought out everything.

"Yes, Mama, I have the bags," I replied, stuffing the money into my shorts.

"Where's your straw hat? It's really hot. You don't want to get burned." Mama knew that I easily burned because of my light complexion and freckles.

"Oh, all right. I'll get it." I didn't mind wearing that straw hat when I worked in the fields on the farm, but I sure hated to wear it when I was around strangers.

"And one more thing—don't race that horse. It's too hot. You'll kill him." Mama looked me straight in the eye to make sure I got the message.

Pulling the jumper with me in it was easy for Billy and he even seemed to enjoy it. That summer morning he could hardly be held back. He broke into an easy trot and I just relaxed the reins and let him have his head and follow the dirt road to Doswell. Occasionally I did rein him in and slow him to a walk so he wouldn't get too hot. I remembered Mama's words, "—-don't race that horse."

When we reached the end of our dirt road with its trees on both sides, we came out on the paved county road that ran through the town of Doswell. Campbell's store was only about a quarter mile down that paved road just before it crossed the RF&P railroad tracks. I drove Billy up to Campbell's Store and tied him up alongside the ice house. I took off that straw hat and strode into the store. A trip to the store was always fun for me. Even if I couldn't buy any of the things, it was fun to look. Campbell's was a general store and it had everything for sale: farm tools, shoes, sugar, coffee, cookware and a thousand other things that fascinated me. Oh, and did he have a selection of candy! The many varieties of candy were in a display case with a glass front. No little fingers messing with that candy. Mama won't mind if I buy just one of those B-B Bat suckers; I thought. They only cost a penny. B-B Bats were long chewy caramel flavored suckers and one of my favorites. If you just sucked on them and didn't bite off the end, they lasted a long time. I stared at the array of candy for several minutes trying to decide which I wanted.

"What can I get you, young man?" The clerk asked.

"I believe I'll have one of those chocolate B.B.Bat suckers. That one right there," I said, pointing to the box of candy.

"Anything else?" The clerk was patient but he knew I probably had been sent to buy things other than that sucker.

"Oh, yes. Mama wants fifty pounds of ice. We're going to make ice cream tomorrow. My sister and her family are coming up from Richmond."

The clerk helped me wrap the block of ice in the three burlap sacks and put it in the basket of the jumper. Holding my sucker in my left hand and the reins in my right, I headed Billy back home. My feet rested on the block of ice because there wasn't any other place. It felt deliciously cold. Already the burlap bags were getting damp and I knew the ice was starting to melt. I needed to hurry on back home. Billy was well rested and soon broke into a nice canter as we headed down the dirt road toward our farm. He actually seemed to enjoy running if he was not tired. I wondered if he had been bred and trained to be a riding horse, maybe even a race horse. I could imagine being in one of those sulky races with a fancy green and yellow uniform and a jaunty yellow jockey's cap. I let my imagination wander and with slight snap of the reins on Billy's back he picked up his gait a little. The jumper was light, even with me and the ice, and it was no strain for a horse to pull. I imagined I could hear the crowd cheering as we rounded the final turn of the race track and I gave Billy another tap with the reins and he responded with a real spurt of speed. Boy, we're really going now! We came to a curve in the road where there was always sand and the jumper actually skidded a bit but Billy kept up his fast trot. Just as we came out of the curve, Billy gave a loud groan and collapsed with his front legs extended in front of him. The stays of the jumper dug into the dirt stopping quickly and I was pitched forward out of the jumper and onto Billy. I landed on his back face down and rolled off into the dirt. Billy tried to get up, but couldn't, and just rolled over on his side. He was breathing heavily and moaning softly every once in a while. I dusted the dirt off my clothes as I stood looking at Billy lying there. What had happened? I knew I had been running the horse but——— Then I remembered the words Mama had cautioned me with when I left home, "Now, LeRoy, don't race that horse."

I was really scared now. Maybe Billy was going to die. I noticed he was sweating pretty hard also. I guess I didn't realize how hard I'd been pushing him. I was in some kind of a fix now! Mama and Daddy are really going to be mad. I'd better see if I can get Billy up. He was tangled by the harness and so I first got him unhitched. Then I pushed the jumper back out of the way. I pulled on the bridle and called to him, "Come on, Billy. Get up. Get up." He tried once but didn't make it. I tugged on the bridle some more calling out to him, "Come on, Boy. Get up."

This time he responded and with a great sigh suddenly came up on all fours. He gave himself a shake to get off some of the dirt and stood there looking dazed as if he also wondered what had happened. Boy, he was a mess with dirt stuck on him and all that sweat. I had to get him cleaned up someway. I didn't have a cloth or brush or anything. Then I thought of the burlap sacks wrapped around the ice. I tipped up one end of the block of ice and slipped off one of the sacks. I guess that cool wet sack felt good on Billy as I wiped him down. In a few minutes he was switching off the flies with his long tail and seemed all right. I hitched him up and got back into the jumper and started home. This time there was no running, just a nice walk. There was a small creek that flowed across the road and I let Billy drink as much as he wanted. He was getting cooled down now and still had some dirt on his side where he rolled over. So while he was drinking out of the creek, I finished wiping him down and then tossed the dirty burlap bag into the bushes. I checked myself and dusted off my clothes and my legs and arms. Mama won't notice a little dirt. I was making up excuses why we were so long coming home and then I suddenly realized I didn't have my straw hat. Guess I lost it when I got pitched out of the jumper back there. Oh well, I'll just say I must have left it at Campbell's Store.

"What took you so long, LeRoy? Why half the ice is melted! I hope we have enough to make ice cream tomorrow," Mama complained as I put the ice in the spring house.

I thought it wise not to even get into a discussion so I just didn't respond and mumbled something about having to go feed and water the chickens and collect the eggs. No one ever knew of my accident with Billy. I don't know if it was just exhaustion or maybe it was a slight heart attack. He was with us for years after that and seemed all right. But you can bet that I never ran him again. Every time I hitched up Billy, I remembered those words of Mama's, "Now, LeRoy, don't race that horse."

The Ram

Our small flock of sheep had one ram and about a couple dozen ewes. We sheared the wool from the sheep in the spring. For some reason we never ate any of the sheep or lambs. Sheep have to be pastured carefully and moved from one pasture to another or they will eat the grass down to the roots and kill it. Of course, if you have a large lush pasture with plenty of grass then there is little problem. One of my jobs was to herd the sheep to and from the barn to the pasture just down the hill from the barn. It was the same pasture that Emil Brenckman landed his biplane in when I was a young boy.

"LeRoy, you'd better get those sheep in to the barn. It's looking like a rain is coming this afternoon," Daddy instructed as he led the cows into the barn.

The sky was darkening and it was nearly sundown that spring day. I hurried down the hill toward the pasture. Now, sheep are funny animals; I thought they were the dumbest animals on our farm. All you had to do was get one of them headed toward the barn and the rest would follow. But if there was a ram in the flock, he would normally take the lead and the ewes would follow. In fact, until the ram led the way the others just milled about aimlessly and it was nearly impossible to get them headed toward the barn. So my technique was to single out the ram and head him toward the barn. That's what I did this afternoon. For some reason, the ram was in a nasty mood and didn't want to lead his flock out of the pasture. He stood between me and the other sheep and moved about nervously as if he wasn't sure what he wanted to do. I shouted at him, waved my arms and moved in closer in an attempt to head him toward the gate and out of the pasture. Suddenly he stopped moving about, put his head down and came rushing directly at me.

When I came to, I was lying on my back looking up at the sky and the clouds passing over. I tried to call out but there was no sound. My head was swimming some and I felt as if the ground was moving. I repeatedly tried to make a sound but I had no voice. In a minute or so, the pasture stopped moving about and I made a feeble call, "Help!"

No one heard me. I sat up and realized what had happened. The ram had run at me and butted me in the stomach knocking all the wind out of me. I was still too dizzy to stand but I noticed the sheep were all gone. Then I heard Daddy call me from the barn, "LeRoy, where are you? Get up here and help me get these sheep in the barn." I got up and staggered up to the barn.

By the time I met Daddy at the back of the barn he had the sheep in and was puzzled about where I had been.

"What happened to you?" He asked.

"That old ram butted me in the stomach and knocked me down."

"Oh, so that's why you didn't come up with the sheep. I wondered where you had gone. Sometimes that old ram gets mean. Now here's what you do next time. Take this pitchfork with you and don't let him scare you. Let him know you're the boss and make him lead those sheep out. Do you understand? Now dust off your clothes and go to the house and wash up for supper," Daddy instructed.

The next day I followed Daddy's instructions and took the pitchfork with me when I went down to bring in the sheep. The situation was the same as the day I got butted: the ram refused to lead the sheep out and paced about nervously while looking toward me. I was scared but I remembered Daddy's words and held the pitchfork in front of me like a spear. Suddenly I saw the ram lower his head and charge toward me. I pointed the pitchfork directly at him and braced myself. He apparently did not see the pitchfork and plunged headlong into it. I was knocked back but didn't lose my balance. The four tine pitchfork caught him squarely on that bony part of his face. Two tines on each side were spread enough so he only got a scrape on each cheek. An inch one way or the other and he could have been speared or even lost an eye. I don't know who was the most startled. I was shaking from fright, but I yelled at him and he backed off and trotted toward the gate. The other sheep followed him up to the barn.

I never went down in that pasture again to get the sheep without my pitchfork. It was a hard lesson for that ram to learn, but from that day on he knew who was "boss."

Ol' Rooster

It seems to me I had the job of looking after the chickens for ever! I know I was pretty young, probably about the time I started school in the second grade. That would make me seven years old. The worst time was in the winter when you had to break the ice in the watering pans and then fill them with hot water brought from the kitchen. Gathering the eggs in the afternoon was always fun. Besides eating a lot of eggs, they were a source of money when we sold them to Campbell's Store in Doswell. Not a lot of money, but a welcome source of exchange for some sugar or maybe a pound of coffee.

As was the practice, we had one rooster with our flock of hens. That rooster liked to strut about and flap his wings and try to scare me whenever I went into the pen to tend to the chickens. He was a large Rhode Island Red with a big spur on each leg. I was afraid of him and was careful not to turn my back on him. One day I entered the chicken yard and was putting some water in the pans and I forgot to watch for that rooster. As I bent over to fill the water pans, he flew up on my back and I felt his sharp spurs dig into my back. I whirled around, threw him off and quickly ran for the gate. I was more scared than hurt, but when I got back to the house I was sobbing and complaining to Mama.

"That ol' rooster just jumped on my back and stuck his spurs in me! I'm not going back in that chicken pen again—ever," I sobbed.

"Now, LeRoy, it's not that bad. Come here and let me see where you're hurt," Mama said, hugging me. "Oh, it's just a scratch. I'll put some iodine on it and you'll be all right."

Iodine was Mama's universal cure-all. She used it on all cuts, bites, scratches and whatever. At my outcry that, "It stings, it hurts, it burns, Mama. Please don't put any more on... Oh, it hurts so bad!!"

Her calm reply would be, "Oh, now, LeRoy, it's not that bad. It'll stop stinging in a minute. The stinging is what kills the germs and keeps that scratch from getting infected."

Whether or not she was medically correct I don't know, but I know that I had many cuts, scratches and bites that never developed into anything serious. Oh, but I hated those treatments with iodine!

Mama had another treatment for chest colds, sore throats or whooping cough. It was a product called Musterole. She would rub in on my chest and throat and the effect was similar to a muster plaster, which was another old time treatment. Musterole came in a small jar or tube and was a salve. Its principal ingredients were oil of mustard, menthol and camphor. It would turn the skin of your chest red, just like a sunburn. But the most disagreeable characteristic was the searing odor which burned your nasal passages as it was being applied. It was another treatment that was effective, but I also hated it.

Mama used to say, "Now, LeRoy, hold this handkerchief over your nose and close you eyes while I rub this on your chest. It'll only take a minute."

Well, it took longer than a minute and that burning smell came right through the handkerchief. I always held my breath as long as I could but it was never long enough.

When Mama had finished the iodine application to the rooster scratches on my back, she held me in a tight hug for several minutes until I got my sobbing under control. Then she held me at arms length and said quietly, "Now here's what you do. When you go into the chicken pen next time, take a switch, a small branch, and hit it on the ground a few times as you get close to the chickens. Watch the rooster and if he starts to raise his wings and stick out his neck, just bang that stick down on the ground toward him a couple times. Let him know you mean business. He'll leave you alone. Now, can you do that?"

"Yes, Mama, but—-

"No buts, LeRoy, you're a big boy now and that's your job. Everyone has to do their own job or else we'd never get finished. Do you understand?" Mama was quietly reminding me of the fact that everyone on the farm had work to do and no one was allowed to skip their assigned job. I wiped my runny nose and teary eyes on my sleeve and nodded that I understood.

The next day I reluctantly approached the chicken pen with the bucket of feed. Just as I started to open the gate, I remembered Mama's instructions. I looked about but I didn't see anything that would make a good switch. There was a piece of firewood lying on the bottom edge of the wire fencing, probably put there to keep the chickens from getting out. I picked it up and entered the pen with my feed bucket in my left hand and the stick in my right. Sure enough, the rooster came forward out of the flock and raised his wings and stuck out his neck in a menacing way. I was both scared and mad and without a further thought, I hurled the stick straight at the rooster. It struck him in his outstretched neck and knocked him back about three feet. He lay completely still. I thought I might have killed him. Boy, would I be in trouble! Our only rooster! I approached him carefully but he was quiet. Maybe I just knocked him out like the time the ram butted me. I picked him up and sloshed him up and down a couple times in the water pan and then he began to move his legs. I put him down on the dirt and he got up and staggered off wobbling from side to side. In a couple minutes he appeared all right but he stayed away from me over against the far fence. I think I had taught him a lesson although what I did wasn't exactly what Mama had suggested. I certainly got his attention and his respect from that day on.

The Bootlegger

Prohibition was not repealed until 1933. I had heard my parents talk of a bootlegger's still off to the south of our dirt road to Doswell. Nothing was ever said that gave any hint of the location but of course I was cautioned never to go off our property in that direction. They need not have worried; I was not about to go off trying to find a bootlegger's still. In fact, as I walked that road back and forth to Doswell, I sometimes thought I heard noises off in the woods in that general direction and you can bet I quickened my pace. There was a stretch of road with three foot high banks on each side and a heavy growth of tall oak trees on both sides of the road. Except in the middle of the day when the sun was overhead, these trees shaded the road and made it feel sort of like a tunnel. It was always a bit scary to me when I passed through this section and I walked as rapidly as I could. A half mile farther on I would break out of the woods and into the open fields of our farm. That was always a good feeling. Of course, at that point I could see our farmhouse and felt more comfortable.

One day I overheard my Daddy talking to Leonard Cannon, our neighbor from the next farm, about someone getting shot. Then I heard the term "bootlegger" in the conversation. My ears really picked up. That night at supper I asked Daddy what the conversation was about that mentioned "bootlegger" and "someone getting shot." He didn't know a lot of details, just what the neighbors had told him. A man had been killed with a shotgun in our woods, not far off that road I walked to school. I was fascinated in a morbid sort of way. Apparently, there had been some sort of dispute over the bootleg whiskey operation and a man was murdered. Nothing like this had ever happened in our area.

"Did you see the man that was killed?" I asked Daddy.

"Of course not, the sheriff removed the body a couple days ago," Daddy replied.

"But you know where he was killed, don't you?" I pressed for more details.

"Now, LeRoy, that's enough talk about this at the supper table," Mama injected.

"Yes, Ma'am. I just wondered where it was. Daddy, will you show me the place tomorrow?"

The next day Daddy walked with me along the road a short distance into the woods from our field. Only about one hundred feet off the road was a big white oak tree with some heavy brush surrounding it.

The tree was splattered with blood as were the leaves on the ground. It must have been an "execution style" killing. I was both horrified and fascinated. I had seen pictures in the newspaper and Life Magazine of gangster killings in Chicago and other cities, but this was in real color right here on our farm. I couldn't get that sight of all that blood out of my mind for a long time. In fact, several nights I had bad dreams remembering that bloodied tree.

I had to pass that spot each day as I walked to and from school. It always gave me a little shiver, particularly if it was late in the day. My walk always quickened until I broke out of the woods into our field and could see our house. Then I felt safe.

The Hurricane of 1933

Aunt Melissa, we called her Aunt Lissa, was my father's only sister. She was married to John Watkins and they had two sons, Latimer and Roland. Latimer and Roland were about same age as my older sisters, Thelma and Clara. The Watkins lived in the same house in Maryland where Mama and Daddy lived before they moved to Doswell. In August, 1933, Daddy got word that Aunt Lissa had died. At the time Miss Taylor, a long time friend of Mama's from Washington, D.C., was visiting us on the farm. Since we had no car, Janice and Carl offered to take Mama and Daddy up to Maryland to Aunt Lissa's funeral. Miss Taylor agreed to stay with all the children. That would be Janice's children, Evelyn, Roger and Gretchen, and at our house, Robert, Margaret, Emil and me. Of course, I thought it would be great fun to have Janice's children to play with for a few days.

A day after Mama and Daddy left, clouds began to gather and darken. By nightfall the clouds became ominous and there was a stillness in the atmosphere. Robert remarked at supper that it looked like a heavy rain or storm might be coming. All of us children were having too much fun playing to bother about such things. By bedtime, the wind had started to rise and a little rain was falling. Because we had Miss Taylor, a guest, she had one bedroom and the rest of us crowded up the best we could. Roger, Gretchen and I all piled into one bed together. Even with the wind rising and the rain pelting on the windowpanes, we were having a good time talking until we finally fell asleep.

What we didn't know was that a hurricane was headed our way. After a long trail across the Atlantic, the hurricane made landfall in the Nags Head area and moved in a northwest direction across Norfolk and headed for Washington. Winds were in the 70 to 80 mph velocity. The winds caused the Potomac River to crest 12 feet above normal, flooding parts of Alexandria, Virginia, and Washington, D.C. From Washington the storm maintained its intensity and headed north bringing it close to the Doswell area. Wind velocities must have been eighty to ninety miles per hour when it passed our farm.

Sometime in the early hours of the morning, I awoke to hear a great roaring of the wind and rain slashing at the windows. Occasionally we heard the crack of a tree limb as it failed to resist the powerful wind and crashed down in our yard. By that time everyone was awake and lights appeared in the living room and kitchen. Then over the roar of the wind, we head a bumping sound coming from the back of the house. At first we thought it might be a tree limb banging on the roof. Robert went out of the kitchen to the adjoining back room, where we kept our washing machine, firewood and old clothes and boots, to see if he could locate the source of the banging. He was quickly met by rain coming into the room from a gap where the roof joined the back wall. The roof was actually banging up and down by the wind, letting rain into the back room. By this time everyone was up and afraid the storm was going to destroy our house. Miss Taylor tried to calm us children, but I could tell the way her hands shook that she was more frightened than we were. She lived in the city and I doubt she had ever experienced anything like this. Once I saw her kneel down on the rug near the fireplace and bow her head in prayer. Miss Taylor was a Roman Catholic and she took her religion seriously. I was scared enough that I thought a prayer might be a good idea.

Robert called to Emil to come to the back room where he was. "Emil, I see what the problem is. The roof has broken loose on that far corner and that's where the rain is pouring in. If we had some way to tie the roof down, we could keep the rain out."

"There's some rope in the barn. I'll go get it," Emil yelled over the storm's fury.

"No, you stay here with the kids. I'll go."

Robert put on an old coat and a hunting cap and headed out the door. The wind was really howling and banged the kitchen screen door back against the house breaking one of the hinges. It was black outside and Robert quickly disappeared in the dark on his way to the barn. He had no lantern; the wind would have blown it out it seconds. We waited anxiously for a long time and began to think something might have happened to him. But after a while, he returned looking like the proverbial "drowned rat." He had brought a coil of rope.

"Get that short ladder up near the corner so we can put this rope around one of rafters and see if we can tie it down," Robert yelled to Emil.

The section of the roof was further loosened by the wind and more rain was pouring in. The combination of the roaring wind and the banging of the loose roof was deafening.

"There's nothing I can tie the rope to. I've got to get the rope around a rafter. Gimme that hammer and I'll see if I can knock a hole up here between the rafter and the roof," Emil called down.

Emil banged away for several minutes before he had a small hole big enough to pass the rope through and over the rafter. He was thoroughly soaked from the rain by this time.

"Tie off the rope and come down and help me pull the roof down," Robert yelled.

Together they pulled the roof down and closed off most of the space where the rain was pouring in so hard. By the time they secured the roof it became just a little lighter outside signaling that day was breaking.

"Now, children, you go on back to bed. It's too early to get up. I think the storm is passing. You can sleep for a while. I'll call you when it's time for breakfast," Miss Taylor assured us.

The wind was easing a bit but none of us could go back to sleep.

We had had a harrowing night. It was a storm to remember. I certainly never forgot it.

Washed Out

Depending on the weather, washing clothes was traditionally a Monday job. We had a hand powered washing machine with a hand crank wringer mounted on top of it which we kept in that unfinished room just off the kitchen. The tub of the washing machine was made of wooden staves, sort of like a barrel, except the sides were straight. The dasher inside was also of wood and through a series of gears was connected to a wooden lever on the outside of the tub. The lever was vertical and you moved it back and forth to actuate the dasher, thereby washing the clothes. When the clothes were washed, they could be run through the ringer which was turned by the crank handle. Then the dirty water was drained from the washer into buckets and emptied outside. Clean water was then added and the clothes run through another cycle to rinse them. Finally, after the rinse they could be rung out and then taken outside and hung on the clothes lines in the backyard. Washing was a major exercise; there were lots of dirty clothes from all of us on the farm.

Often, but not always, Mama would have Mary Cannon from the adjoining farm come over to help with the washing. Mary was a woman in her forties and she had a daughter, Marjory, about my age. So when Mary came over with Marjory, I had some one to play with for the morning. On this day, however, Mama said Mary Cannon could not come and that I would have to help her with the washing.

" I need you to run the washer for me. I've put in the soap already so just put in that pile of overalls and socks and start washing."

"Aw, gee. Do I have to? I was just gonna fly my airplane," I complained.

Working that washing machine was not one of my favorite things. It always seemed to happen when I was in the middle of some play activity. The good thing was I could just dream and make believe while

I worked that lever back and forth. I didn't have to think about what I was doing.

As usual on wash days, Mama had a big pile of dirty clothes there on the floor behind me. I knew I was in for a lot of washing. I was thinking about cowboys and horses and roping and stuff as I worked the drive lever back and forth. The next thing I remembered was Mama calling me from a long ways away, like she was outdoors.

"LeRoy, are you tending that washer? Doesn't sound like you're working it. LeRoy, answer me. Are you all right?"

I opened my eyes and the room seemed to be rotating slowly about me. I could see the ceiling of the room and realized I was lying on my back. I tried to answer Mama, but no sound came out. I felt dizzy and really confused.

Next, I heard Mama's voice again and then saw her face close to mine and she said, "LeRoy, what are you doing lying down there in that pile of dirty clothes?"

"I— I— don't know," I whispered. I was still confused and dizzy as Mama pulled me up to a sitting position. "What happened?" She asked as she stooped down beside me.

After a long pause, I said, "I think I hit my elbow on the doorframe there. But I don't remember."

"You probably hit your funnybone and fainted. Here, let me see your elbow. No, not that one, the other one. There's a place where the skin is broken and it's bleeding a little. I think that's what happened. How do you feel now? Can you get up?"

"I guess so but I'm still a little dizzy," I answered as Mama put her arm around me and helped me up.

"You come in the kitchen and sit down and I'll go get the iodine to put some on your elbow," Mama said.

I hated it when she put that iodine on a cut. It stung something awful, but that was Mama's standard treatment for any cut. I thought after this experience that Mama would let me off from the washing job, at least for today. But she had other plans.

"Now, that will fix up your elbow and keep it from getting infected," she said, giving me a hug. "Just sit here a few minutes and then you can go back and finish running the washing machine."

I grumbled about having to go back and run that washing machine but I knew Mama would not let me off. Mama was insistent that "a job assigned meant a job that had to be completed."

14

The Family

Ancestry

An excellent genealogy of the Day family is contained in the book: "James Day of Browningsville and His Descendants", by Jackson H. Day, February 1976. Excerpts from this book which cover the line of our family: John Day, James Day, Luther Day, Rufus King Day, Latimer Day (my grandfather), and Ira Day (my father) are contained in the Appendix. The Appendix contains some interesting aspects of the life of James Day including his time as a soldier in the Revolutionary War, his involvement in the Methodist Church and the freeing of his slaves. There are other branches of the Day family and relations not contained in the Appendix which are fully detailed in Jackson Day's book. These farming families tended to have a large number of children. My grandfather, Latimer W. Day, came from a family of ten children, six of them boys. Latimer W. Day married Venia Browning and their two children were Ira Eugene (my father) and Melissa (my Aunt Lisa). My immediate family consisted of eight children, four boys and four girls. I was the youngest of the eight.

Family Members

Sallie Lester Day (Mama) 1881-1963

My mother was born and raised in Richmond, Virginia. She was forty-three years old when I was born so my earliest memory of her was when she was in her late forties. Pictures of her, when she was about twenty, show a beautiful young woman, tall and slender with auburn hair piled up on her head. She had done very well in high school, as attested by a letter of high recommendation given by the principal, Mr. Leroy Edwards. Mama had gone on to normal school and became a teacher. She greatly admired Mr. Edwards and told me that I was named after him. She was very quick in mathematics, well read and loved conversation with others. She had a positive outlook on life and even in advanced years when she had more than the usual "aches and pains of old age," she seldom complained. In our household she was the organizer, the planner, the one who took care of the sick, the teacher, the money manager (what little we had)—all of these things in addition to being the mother to eight children as well as the housekeeper. In times of need she even helped with the farming. We never had any help in the house except sometimes Mary Cannon, from the neighboring farm, who came over to help Mama with the washing on Mondays. I think Mama hired her partly just because she felt sorry for her and would give her a dollar or so for helping. Of course, in earlier times, Mama had help from my older brothers and sisters when they were still home. During those years when she was in her thirties, she even tackled the hard farming jobs with the help of my older brother, Randolph, when Daddy was sick for a period. She could handle a team of horses as well as she could bake a batch of biscuits.

Mama set the moral tone for my brothers and sisters. She made it very clear what was right and what was wrong. She instilled in me the curiosity to learn, to do a job well and completely, and to be considerate of others. I remember her sitting with me and guiding me in my school homework and encouraging me to do my best in whatever I undertook. She was an avid reader and our house always had books. I know my love of reading was inspired by her. I had several serious illnesses when I was a child, including pneumonia and whooping cough. I loved it when she would come and sit by my bed and read stories to me. I particularly remember one book she gave me. It was an oversized book called "The Great Explorers." Each page was devoted to one of the early explorers: Magellan, Columbus, Sir Francis Drake, DeSoto, Henry Hudson and all the rest. The book was illustrated with color pictures depicting some aspect of each of the explorers. I loved to read that book and imagine myself aboard one of those ships sailing away to discover new places.

I loved my mother dearly and I know she loved me, too. She was not overly affectionate but I can remember many times when she gave me a hug or a kiss as a reward for a job well done, or at times when we said good-bye when I went to visit my older sister, Janice, for a few days. In those days it was not customary to show too much affection between parents and children. But there were many ways she made me feel loved. I know she loved all of her children and had devoted her life to making a good home for our family under very difficult circumstances. In my case, she stressed many times the importance of "making something of myself." All of my brothers and sisters had left the farm when they finished their schooling and had done well with their careers in Richmond. Mama wanted me to do as well or better.

Ira Eugene Day (Daddy) 1879-1955

Daddy was born and raised on my grandfather's farm near Kemptown, Maryland. He attended the Kemptown School but only went through the sixth grade. This was customary for boys who were going to farm. He was working on the farm when he met my mother, Sallie Lester, and married her in 1902; he was twenty-three. In fact, after they were married they lived in a house on my grandfather's farm and Daddy continued to help my grandfather run the farm.

Daddy was of medium height, with black hair and a complexion that tanned readily from the sun. I remember his muscles were hard as wood from the years of work on the farm. He could saw wood or pitch hay or shovel sand into our wagon for hours without ever complaining of being tired. When I first remember him, he was about fifty and he rose at dawn and could work a long day of manual tasks. The work on our farm was especially hard because we only had two pieces of mechanized equipment: a small gasoline engine that pumped the water from the well to the house and another larger gasoline engine that powered a circular saw which Daddy used to cut up wood for the kitchen cook stove, the fireplace and the furnace in the cellar. Without a tractor, all the farm work was done with our two horses and the mule. Until we bought our first car in 1936, our transportation was by the farm wagon or the one-horse jumper that I liked to drive. When I was growing up, Daddy had no hired help with the farming. Certain tasks had to be done every day: taking care of the stock and milking the one or two cows were typical. Therefore, he never took off any time.

Many times I wished we could have had electricity in our house like they had in the town of Doswell. High voltage transmission lines crossed our farm running on that slope below the barn and the lower pasture. So close and yet so far as any help to us. With only one other house on the road to Doswell besides us, there was no economic justification for bringing electricity the two miles to our farm.

My beloved mother, who guided me and
inspired me to reach for lofty goals.

My daddy, taken long after I left the farm. Circa 1946.

Daddy was not a book reader like Mama. He read magazines, particularly those that dealt with agricultural themes. Whenever we had a newspaper, he read that from front to back. He was not the conversationalist that Mama was. Understandably, he was usually the first to go to bed and the first one up in the morning.

He was good to me; I never got a whipping from him. Oh, there were times when he was frustrated by things like my clumsiness in guiding the horses to cultivate the garden. My job was to ride the horse and guide him so as not to trample the rows of beans or tomatoes while Daddy steered the cultivator. Often I lost my concentration by thinking of some play activity and allowed the horse to step into the vegetable rows. But in times of frustration with me or the horses or cows, I never heard him lash out with profanity. He would yell at me or them, but I never heard him curse. Profanity or vulgar language was never used in our home. For that I am grateful.

Daddy was most comfortable discussing the weather or the crops or the animals with a neighbor farmer or the local storekeeper in Doswell. He loved to show the crops to my older brothers and sisters when they came up from Richmond on Sundays. These were the fruits of his labor and he was understandable proud of them. Besides, it was probably easy for him to relate to his adult children who had worked beside him for years on the farm.

I didn't have as close a relationship with Daddy as I had with Mama. He was certainly not the affectionate type, and gave no hugs or pats on the back. But in those days it was not customary to show that type of affection. I never saw him give my mother a hug, either, but I know he cared for her. Overall, he and I had a good relationship that allowed us to work together but it was not the loving one I had with my mother. He taught me many things: how to saddle up a horse, milk a cow (though he insisted that was his job), how to deal with the animals, how to saw a log with a crosscut saw, how to drive a team of horses and countless other tasks so central to life on the farm. He showed me how to carve with a knife without cutting myself, how to fell a tree and make it fall where you wanted it to—all these things came naturally as the jobs presented themselves in the course of doing the farm work. Most of all, he taught me that there was satisfaction and dignity in doing physical work although it might seem onerous at the time.

Janice Louise Day 1904 - 1997

Janice was the oldest of the eight children in our family. She was twenty-one when I was born and helped in my delivery there on the farm according to what Mama told me. Janice was born in Maryland while Mama and Daddy lived in the house on Grandfather's farm. She was eight before they moved from Maryland down to the farm at Doswell. Because she had gone to school in Kemptown, Maryland, she knew a lot of the people up there and always had a strong attachment to our Maryland relatives and friends. While she lived on Grandfather's farm, she and Grandmother Day developed a close relationship. She spent quite a lot of time over in the big house. Grandmother Day taught her lots of cooking tricks. Janice always admired the gravy that Grandmother made and one day she asked Grandmother to teach her how to make it. The secret according to Grandmother Day was to put the flour in a measuring cup and add a couple tablespoons of water and stir until all the lumps were gone. Then this mixture was stirred into the meat juice and the result was a smooth gravy without any lumps. Janice never forgot this trick and added it to the cooking skills which Mama taught her. As she grew, she developed exceptional cooking skills.

One of the reasons why Janice knew so many people in and around Kemptown was because of the "Wednesday social outings" that she took with Grandmother Day. Wednesday afternoons were the times that Grandmother Day typically went out to visit friends and relatives. She would often ask Janice if she would like to come along. Of course, Janice was delighted. Mama would dress Janice in her "Sunday dress." Then Grandmother would drive by with the horse and buggy, pick up Janice and they would be off for an afternoon of visiting. Janice loved it and never forgot all the people she visited on those "Wednesday social outings."

Being the oldest, Janice was a great help to Mama with the younger children. She was eleven when my brother, Robert, was born. She was especially fond of caring for him when he was a baby. One day she and Mama had an argument and Janice decided she was going to run away from home and take Robert with her. Robert, at the time, was only a few months old. She dressed him in his best baby dress complete with his fancy cap with a ruffle that tied under his chin and put him in the baby carriage. Without saying anything to anyone, she rolled the carriage down the hill near the barn and onto the flats below the house. Of course, shortly Mama discovered that both Janice and the baby were gone and saw Janice rolling the carriage along the road toward the river. Daddy went after her and talked her into returning home. Janice loved to tell this story on herself.

Because there was no suitable high school close to Doswell, Mama and Daddy arranged for Janice to live with Grandmother West, Mama's maternal grandmother, in Richmond, in order to go to high school. When she finished high school, she went to work at the Life Insurance Company of Virginia. She only worked there a short time but long enough to become a member of the company softball team. At seventeen years old she married Carl Pflugradt, who had lived on the adjoining farm, Bullfield.

Janice, as the oldest of the Day children, was a generation away from me. However, I had a very close relationship with her and her family.

She learned about hard work at an early age. She became a strong woman, both morally and physically. As a result of living on the farm, she had a great interest in growing things. Even when she and Carl lived in Richmond and their children were small, she found time to have a garden. When she and her family came up to the farm on Sundays, I often saw her walking with Daddy along the edges of the fields talking about the crops. She was a good cook and always baked all their own bread. She called it graham bread, a version of whole wheat bread. I know she learned bread baking from Mama because we always had home baked bread.

Their three children, Evelyn, Roger and Gretchen, were about my age and became my playmates. Although they lived in Richmond, they usually visited us on the farm about every other Sunday. Because Janice was the oldest and I was the youngest, she was really a generation from me. She was like another "mother" to me. We had an especially close relationship, closer than I had with any of my other sisters or brothers.

Many times she and Carl invited me to visit her family and those stays in Richmond away from the farm were a great treat for me.

Claude Randolph Day 1906 - 1973

Like Janice, Randolph was also born in Kemptown, Maryland. He was only six years old when Mama and Daddy moved to Doswell so he had less of an attraction to the people in Maryland than Janice. Randolph always had a jolly disposition. While my other brothers were reserved, he was always outgoing, always joking and laughing. His conversation lit up the room. When Randolph left the farm to find work in Richmond, he jokingly said, "After I get a job in Richmond, I am going to eat roast beef and mash potatoes as often as I want." No doubt this remark referred to some of the lean times on the farm but I doubt that he ever went hungry. Perhaps it was just an expression of the freedom he expected. In any event, his brothers and sisters kidded him about that remark for years. Well, perhaps he did eat as much as he wanted because I remember him being heavier than any of my lean brothers and sisters.

When Randolph was still in high school, he became interested in trapping animals and curing the hides. Of course, the wild animals he could trap on our farm were limited to rabbits, squirrels and an occasional fox. His interest was probably stimulated by an ad in the back of "Popular Mechanics" magazine telling how you could make good money by selling hides of animals that you had trapped. This interest in furs led him to a job with the Henry Hasse Fur Company when he moved to Richmond. That company manufactured and sold all sorts of fur garments. Randolph became an expert fur cutter and continued with the Hasse Fur Company until he retired.

After Randolph had joined the Hasse Fur Company in Richmond and made a little money, he had the idea to raise muskrats on our farm. He and Daddy and my brother, Robert, laid out an area on the far corner of our farm where there was a creek that would supply the necessary water. Enclosing the area with fence so the muskrats could not escape was the difficult job. Muskrats could burrow under any normal fence and escape. The fence had to be sunk about a foot into the ground and further protected with sheet metal below the ground level to keep the muskrats from escaping. For a time, we had a number of muskrats but the endeavor was never successful and before long they all escaped. The muskrat pen, which became know as the "zoo," was an attraction for visitors but it never was a source of income.

Alberta and Randolph Day. A visit to Hilldene, winter 1929.

Randolph married Alberta Mehl, whom we all called "Berta." Berta was friendly to everyone and a favorite at our house. She took a lot of ribbing when the crowd went down to the North Anna River for a Sunday swim because Berta was not a swimmer. However, she was a good sport and would spend most of the time on the little sandy shore of the river while the rest of us frolicked in the water. In our family we always referred to the swimming hole at the river as "Berta's Beach." Randolph and Alberta had no children.

Thelma Lester Day 1910 - 1997

Like Janice and Randolph, Thelma was also born in Kemptown, Maryland, but she was too young to remember much before the move to the farm at Doswell in 1913. When she was eight years old, she became sick with the disease called Lupus. Lupus is a chronic disease that causes inflammation and pain in the joints. I am sure not much was known about it in those days. Furthermore, this was the time when Daddy was so sick with the influenza and Mama, with the help of Randolph, had to carry on the farming. Probably Mama feared that Thelma might contract the sickness that Daddy had and further complicate her condition. So they decided to send her up to spend a year with Grandmother Day in Maryland. Thelma attended the third grade at the Kemptown Grammar School. Our cousin, Latimer Watkins, remembers walking to school with her. In the year she spent with Grandmother Day, she got to know a lot of the people there in the Kemptown area. When she was grown, she often visited these friends and relatives she had gotten to know as a little girl. The Lupus disease plagued her off and on all her years but it never kept her from an active life.

Thelma left the farm when I was only one or two so I only remember her as an adult. She finished her high school at Varina, on the outskirts of Richmond, Virginia. Like Janice, she had also been sent to the Richmond area for high school. She lived with the Drinker family just outside of Richmond. When she graduated, she went into Richmond to find a job. She worked at Miller and Rhodes Department store; Thalheimers was the other big department store. They were both on Broad Street separated only by 6th Street and they were fierce competitors. Thelma worked her way up from salesgirl to become the buyer for the Ladies Department at Miller and Rhodes. That meant she was the "boss" of that department. Later she went to work at Thalheimers and had an even better job as a buyer of a large department. She was very stylish and meticulously groomed; every strand of her dark hair was in place and set in the style of the day. She had Daddy's complexion and his dark hair.

Thelma and her husband, Raymond Traylor, bought some land at Ellison outside of Richmond and built a nice house where they raised their two children, Forrest and Fay. Thelma and Raymond were founding members of the Cool Springs Baptist Church in Mechanicsville, Virginia, and active in it for many years.

In the times when I visited Janice and her family, Mama would instruct me, "Now, LeRoy, if Janice takes you in town to Richmond, you must be sure to go into Miller and Rhodes and go and speak to your sister, Thelma. You wear that white shirt I put in for you and that nice blue necktie. Janice will help you tie it."

Well, I followed all those instructions and took the elevator to the third floor, Ladies Department. It was embarrassing to walk through all those ladies underwear, nightgowns and stockings to get to the back of the department where I knew Thelma could be found.

"Hi, I'm looking for Mrs. Thelma Day. I'm her brother," I said, fidgeting with my necktie.

"You mean Mrs. Traylor? I can see you must be her brother; you look like her." The saleslady was trying to be polite.

"Yes, Mrs. Traylor."

I had forgotten to use her married name. She had married Raymond Traylor who was the one who set up all those displays in the windows that faced on the street. By that time my face was getting pretty flushed; it was always so embarrassing to come up to this Ladies Department where everything was so fine, so expensive. And that remark that I looked like Thelma. Me, with my red hair and freckles. Why I didn't look anymore like Thelma than a bedpost!

In a minute Thelma came out from the back where she did her book work and said, "LeRoy, come here and let me fix your tie."

She slipped the knot up real tight until I felt like I was being choked. Thelma couldn't tolerate a tie that wasn't cinched up absolutely tight under the collar. This was the standard greeting I got every time I went up to see her in that Ladies Department.

We talked for a few minutes. She asked about Mama and Daddy and how were things going on the farm. After a short time, we ran out of things to say and I told her I had to meet Janice across the street in Thalheimers. We said our goodbyes and I hurried to the elevator. While I waited for the elevator, I loosened that tie just a bit; I was sure Thelma couldn't see me. As the elevator descended to the first floor, I wondered if she might be just a little embarrassed of me. It was probably because she was the boss of that fancy department and I was her little brother off the farm. She seemed so different when she came home to the farm; she was so relaxed and loving to me.

Thelma in her high school graduation dress. June 1928.

Clara Lavinia Day 1913 - 2000

Clara inherited her reddish hair and light complexion from Mama. She was slim and attractive. She always seemed very organized and knew what she wanted to do. Clara also lived with the Drinker family just outside of Richmond while she went to Varina High School for her junior and senior years. She was the Valedictorian of her graduating class of 1931. According to her Senior Yearbook, she was voted by her classmates as "Most Dignified" and "Biggest Bluff."

Clara had many talents ranging from being the manager of the girl's basketball team to writing poetry. The following poem was published in her senior yearbook.

TIES THAT BIND

There is something in being a Senior
That makes our whole hearts glad;
But mingled with all the joy,
There is something that makes us sad.
We think of our graduation,
Of diplomas and all the rest;
But there lies a lump in our throats
That cannot be suppressed.
When we think of the friends we've made,
And how we've strolled the halls,
We are not so eager to leave,
For we know we shall miss it all.
We'll remember the times we were tardy,
How our notes filled up the files!
We will miss those daily frowns,
And of course we'll miss the smiles.
How we led our teachers a chase,
By giggling and talking so!
How they had to change our seats,
From the back to the front of the row.
We never could understand at all,
Why they persistently kept us in,
And why they loved to demerit us,
But we guess we really did sin.
We shall never forget, "Keep quiet, keep still,"
And then "Report to me at recess,"
We feel that without Mr. Baker
Varina could never be,
There's another we'll always remember,
As long years come and pass—

Miss Brooks, so patient and faithful—
The beloved leader of the class.
Now we are all in a fluster,
As we think of our sheep skins so fine!
What a thrill when we feel we can say,
"This High School Diploma is mine!"
All of our lives we've been dreaming;
Now our dream of dreams has come true;
But with all the happiness and joy,
Old Varina, we'll surely miss you."

Clara Day

When she finished high school, Clara enrolled in nurses training at Johnston Willis Hospital in Richmond. She was eighteen years old. The nurse training course was three years and Clara graduated in 1934. A clipping from the Richmond News Leader shows Clara in her nursing uniform holding the first Richmond baby born in 1935. She continued in her nursing career after she was married to Gene Davies. She and Gene Davies had their daughter, Shirley, in 1943. Clara was on duty at Johnston Willis Hospital in 1941 when my brother, Emil, was brought in from a serious motorcycle accident. His leg was badly crushed and Clara thought at the time that he might lose the leg. Fortunately, he did not lose his leg although he was hospitalized for a long time. He went on to serve in the army doing World War II and in the Korean War.

Clara loved music. She learned to play the piano and played almost entirely by "ear." When she would come back to the farm from Richmond on weekends, she would often sit down at our old piano in the living room and play and sing. Soon there was a gathering of other sisters, brothers, girlfriends and boyfriends around the piano for a song fest. Sometimes Albert Dassler, a friend of Randolph's and Janice's, would be there also and he would add to the music by playing his accordion. The old farmhouse was literally ringing with all the music and laughter. Those were good times. Besides playing the piano and singing, Clara loved to dance. Over the years she became an accomplished ballroom dancer.

Clara had a "touch of the farm" in her when it came to growing things. After she was married and had her own home, she always had a yard full of beautiful flowers. Tucked away in some of the tall snapdragons or daisies, would be a couple tomato plants just to provide some tasty delights for the table. She was also a great cook and I remember she made the best fried chicken and biscuits.

Over the years she developed exceptional talents as a seamstress. She could make professional quality drapes and slipcovers. No patterns; just measure, cut, sew and fit. When her daughter, Shirley, was little, she made lots of mother-daughter dresses, identical in every way.

Clara in her new nurse's uniform, Johnston Willis
Hospital, Richmond, Virginia. Circa 1933.

Although Clara gave up her nursing career after many years, the medical experience was valuable in her later work as a medical claims adjuster for the Life Insurance Company of Virginia and later with the Equitable Insurance Company, both in Richmond. She worked for Equitable for many years until her retirement.

Robert Adrian Day 1915 - 2004

Robert had the typical "Day physique", lean and tall. He was quiet, not talkative, just the opposite of Randolph. He loved the farm duties and was a great help to Daddy. He also loved roaming the woods and fields with his dogs hunting for rabbits and squirrels. Whenever Randolph brought his friends up from Richmond to the farm to hunt, Robert was eager and ready to join them. He knew the most likely places they could flush some rabbits.

Like his older brother, Randolph, and his sisters, Robert left the farm after attending Ashland High School and headed to Richmond to find work. It was in the midst of the Great Depression, but he found a job in the Sports Division of Sears, Roebuck and Company. Shortly he moved to the Farm Machinery and Equipment Division and in two years he was promoted to head up the division. Although we never had any of that mechanized equipment on our farm, Robert was quick to become familiar with all of it and to relate easily to the farmers that came in to buy. Within a few years his division was leading in sales.

Not long after Robert and Altah Latham were married, Daddy and Mama gave them a 32 acre section of the farm for a home site. Robert and Altah wanted to build a house there on the western edge of the farm. The 32 acre site included both woods and a portion of the adjoining field. The piece of open land gave them a place to have a garden. Robert dearly loved to grow things and his gardens, in all the places they lived, were highly productive and a thing of beauty. For their home, they designed an authentic log cabin with a big stone fireplace. The logs were cut from trees on the farm. Whenever he had any spare time from his work at Sears and Roebuck, Robert helped in the construction. When the log cabin was completed, they had an attractive house that was rustic on the outside and completely modern on the inside. The house had three bedrooms, one on the first level and two on the upper level. It was their home for about ten years and both of their daughters, Barbara and Roberta, were born there.

While Robert was considered the quietest of the Day children by the family, he was an excellent manager and salesman at Sears and Roebuck. He won many awards for the record sales of his Farm Machinery and Equipment Division where he worked until he retired.

Margaret Antonia Day 1918 - 1998

Margaret had a zest for life. She made friends easily. Her conversation was punctuated with smiles and laughter. But in a twinkle of her eye, she could slip into a pout and show her displeasure with sarcasm. Her personality could best be summed up as "independent." She had a better relationship with Daddy than she had with Mama. For some reason her independent personality clashed with Mama's.

Margaret was smart in school and quick-witted to learn. She was tall and statuesque with beautiful strawberry blond hair. I walked to school with her as far as Doswell, where she caught the bus to take her to high school in Ashland. Often Lucille Cannon from the adjoining Bullfield farm would come over and walk with Margaret. They were in the same grade. Margaret was a fast walker and Emil and I had to hustle to keep up with her and Lucille. Margaret and Lucille kept up a constant chatter about things at school as we hurried along the road to Doswell. I liked to listen to all their conversation and before I realized it we were coming out of the woods and had arrived at Doswell.

*Robert, a successful manager of the Farm Machinery
and Equipment Division of Sears and Roebuck,
brought a bit of the farm with him to the city.
Wherever he lived, he developed a spectacular vegetable
garden that was the pride of the neighborhood.*

*Margaret, not quite sixteen, but she won her diploma
from Ashland High School, Ashland, Virginia. 1934.*

Margaret was not quite sixteen when she graduated from Ashland High School. That summer she announced that she was leaving the farm and going to Richmond to find a job. Everyone was shocked that she was anxious to leave so quickly. Mama felt she was too young to go out on her own and tried to persuade her to stay a year longer on the farm. Margaret would have none of it and angrily argued that there was nothing to keep her on the farm. I remember the argument between Mama and Margaret raged on for hours on one of those hot summer days. Nothing could sway Margaret's mind and in a few days she announced she was leaving that week. She was packed and ready to go when Thelma and Raymond came up on Sunday for their usual visit. On Sunday night she rode back to Richmond with them and began her life of working in the city. She started at Thalheimers Department Store as a salesgirl. Soon, her industry, sales ability and general business sense were recognized. She was promoted and within a couple years Margaret was made the buyer for the Stationery Department. She was one of the youngest buyers in all of Thalheimers.

In her spare time, Margaret became an expert seamstress; she could make anything in the line of clothes. As she grew older, she developed an interest in quilting. Her quilts were a thing of beauty. She gave some to her children and friends but she kept others and they were often displayed for the public. Margaret had quite a reputation for her beautiful quilts.

Margaret visited us on the farm on weekends just like the others who had moved to Richmond. She came up with her boyfriends and later her husband and joined in with the good times we had when the whole family gathered. But she and Mama never regained that close relationship that you want to see between mother and daughter. Her independent spirit just would not compromise. I loved Margaret and she and I had a good relationship. I just wished she and Mama could have reconciled their differences. Margaret had a good career with Thalheimers and distinguished herself by her hard work and likeable personality.

Margaret married Thomas "Buddy" Snead and they had one daughter, Judith. Later they were divorced and she married John Pecawicz. They had two children: Brenda and Alan.

Emil Rodney Day 1921 -

My brother, Emil, is only four years older than I am and therefore we grew up together. Although we played and walked to school together, I still looked up to him as my "big brother." (Even four years difference in age is a lot when you are a child.) We had one common interest that bound us together all our lives: airplanes. When we were boys on the farm, we both built rubber powered model airplanes. These were the stick and tissue ones. I built a high wing model called the Wakefield which was a great flyer. Emil helped me build my first models and showed me how to trim the models so they would climb in a left-hand circle and then glide down in a right-hand circle. We had plenty of space to fly our models, but our favorite spot was out near the barn where we could takeoff and land in the hard packed dirt road.

Emil was full of fun and made friends easily. He also had a mischievous trait which got him into trouble at school sometimes. One time he got a box of the school's cupcakes and went through the lunchroom passing them out to all his friends. The school was not amused and expelled him for a few days. When Emil was in his second year at Ashland High School, he was having some difficulties so Mama and Daddy decided it might be wise for him to attend another school. They sent him to Richmond and he stayed with Clara and attended Thomas Jefferson High School. Thomas Jefferson and John Marshall were the two big city schools. While he attended school he took a job as a night attendant at a gas station. Through his work at the gas station, he became acquainted with some other boys who rode motorcycles. Before long he had saved up enough money to buy his own secondhand Indian motorcycle. About this same time he joined the Virginia National Guard. He also took up flying lessons at a nearby airport. School began to suffer and before long he dropped out.

He continued his night work at the gas station which left his days free. Often he would ride his motorcycle up to the farm for a visit. He would take me for rides on the back of the motorcycle and I thought that was about the most exciting thing I had ever done. I loved the noise and the speed. Later he taught me how to ride the motorcycle by myself. That was a thrill not to be equaled.

As World War II spread in Europe, the training and field maneuvers of the National Guard intensified. By 1941 the National Guard was mobilized into the US Army and Sergeant Day was stationed at Fort Meade, Maryland. In June, 1941, Emil and Henry "Hank" Purvis, one of his riding buddies, were in Richmond on leave and riding on Hank's big Harley Davidson motorcycle. They were struck head-on by a car and both were badly injured. Emil's left leg was so badly crushed that for a while they thought it might have to be amputated. However, after months in the Camp Lee Hospital, he was returned to active duty with the Army.

Later he was shipped overseas and was in Paris soon after its liberation. He was in the Transportation Corp and based at Compiene, north of Paris, during the Battle of the Bulge in December 1944. Emil was a Tech Sergeant at the time but on March 6, 1945 he received a battlefield commission of Second Lieutenant. Less than three weeks later, on March 24, he and a fellow soldier were wounded when their jeep ran over a land mine. Emil was transferred to a hospital in England and then later to a hospital in Augusta, Georgia, for recovery.

After his complete recovery, the Army sent Emil to flight training and he became qualified as a pilot for both fixed wing aircraft and helicopters. During the Korean War he flew helicopters evacuating the wounded back to the Mobile Army Surgical Hospitals (MASH). While he piloted MASH helicopters in Korea, Emil was awarded the Air Medal (second Oak Leaf Cluster) with the following citation:

The President of the United States of America has awarded
The Air Medal, Second Oak Leaf Cluster
To
Captain Emil R. Day, 02011358, Transportation Corps
For
Meritorious Achievement While Participating in Aerial Flight
Korea, 13 October 1952 to 8 January 1953

When he returned to the States, he was a helicopter flight instructor for the Army at Fort Rucker in Alabama. Emil had a distinguished military career and I was always proud of my "big brother."

Emil married Lillian Penny and they had two children, Karen and Rodney. After Lillian's death, he married Opal Hollowell and they have a daughter, Susan.

After Emil left the farm and got a job in Richmond, he would sometimes visit with his motorcycle and give us all a thrilling ride. (l to r) Gretchen, Emil, LeRoy and Roger.

During World War II, Tech Sergeant Emil Day (standing left) hosted a Christmas dinner December 1944 for his outfit in Compiene, France. Shortly thereafter, on March 6, 1945, he received a battlefield commission of Second Lieutenant.

Summing Up

All of my brothers and sisters "made something of themselves" as Mama used to say. Despite the hard work on the farm and the frugal times of the Depression, the Day children had parents that gave them a moral upbringing, a work ethic and a positive outlook on life that served them well all their lives. They all married and had children except Randolph, who had no children. They had respectable careers in spite of the fact that they only had a high school education, with the exception of Clara. Clara had the registered nurse training beyond her high school. They all owned their own homes and none ever fell into personal debt or applied for public assistance. No doubt the frugal times and hard work on the farm as children was beneficial in dealing with life's problems and developing them into responsible adults. There were no drug addicts, no alcoholics and no lawbreakers. Luckily, my parents lived long enough to see them develop into responsible, mature adults.

I know they were proud of all of them.

Emil, a decorated veteran of World War II and the Korean War. In the Korean War, he flew MASH helicopters bringing the wounded soldiers from the battlefield to the field hospital.

15

Farm Farewell

War Clouds

By early 1939 the war clouds in Europe were becoming ominous. German troops had marched into Austria the previous year and declared Austria a state of the German Reich. Austria had offered no resistance; in fact they welcomed the German troops. Austria had a history of anti-Semitism and it flared up quickly when the Nazis moved into Austria. The Nazi SS troops, in plain clothes, initiated riots and encouraged looting and destruction of shops and homes of Jews. All Jews who had been members of the former Austrian government were dismissed. Similarly, professors, editors and other professionals were forced to resign. Persecution of the Jews began immediately; thousands were rounded up for arrest as "undesirables." The people of the United States and other Western countries watched these developments with curiosity and amazement.

After several meetings, Prime Minister Chamberlain of Great Britain and Hitler had signed a peace declaration in September 1938. In this declaration, Germany had pledged not to invade any other countries; however, by March 1939 German troops marched into Czechoslovakia and occupied the country. Obviously, the peace agreement which Chamberlain had promised would "provide peace in our time" was worthless. Tensions in Europe were running high. Also, in March 1939, Prime Minister Chamberlain announced in the House of Commons that Britain and France pledged to provide assistance to Poland in case any other country threatened their independence. In August 1939 this offer was formalized when Great Britain and Poland signed a "mutual assistance" pact. By this time it was becoming clear that Hitler was violating all the peace agreements that had been signed and threatening the whole of Europe.

Isolationism and anti-Semitism were widespread in the United States at this time. Many in the US felt that the problems in Europe were of their own making and that the US should remain neutral. These same people felt that we had rescued Europe in World War I and helped to defeat Germany and we should stay out of it this time. Many politicians and prominent people argued against the United States "getting involved." Of course, there were others who felt we should make special provisions to accept large number of Jews who were trying desperately to get out of Europe. In May 1939 the SS St. Louis left Hamburg with 936 Jewish passengers, mostly from Germany, who hoped to be admitted to the United States. The ship sailed first to Cuba and from there they expected to come to the US. Most of the passengers held papers from the US Immigration Service which they expected would gain them entrance to the US. They went initially to Cuba to wait until the US immigration quotas would allowed them to enter. When the ship reached Havana, they were not allowed to get off the ship. The Cuban authorities said their Visas were no good. Family members and friends who had come to Cuba to meet their loved ones pleaded in vain. The passengers on board, many who had spent their life savings for this escape from the death and destruction going on in Europe, were distraught and panic stricken. Several threatened suicide; one person committed it. Requests to President Roosevelt to intervene and rescue the Jews were turned down. Roosevelt refused because of the strong anti-Semitism in the United States at that time. The ship left Cuba and sailed about on the seas for nearly a month while attempts were made to find some country that would allow the Jews to immigrate. Finally, Belgium agreed that the ship could land there.

From Belgium, the Jews scattered to France, England, Holland and some stayed in Belgium. None of them were allowed into the US where they originally had hoped to go. This was typical of the plight of the Jews at that time; the world was largely indifferent to their persecution.

I was ignorant of all these happenings at the time. I overhead some of the conversation of the adults about "problems in Europe" but they were about places and people foreign to me. I couldn't have found places like Vienna or Berlin or Danzig on a map. We had no radio and only an occasional newspaper, so news of happenings in Europe were pretty much out of mind. Occasionally, when we went to a movie in Ashland, there would be a newsreel that showed some politician making a speech about the situation in Germany or a quick flash of German troops marching. It made little impression on me; I was impatiently waiting for the main feature to begin with Wallace Berry, Will Rogers or Gene Autrey.

In the spring of '39, I was concentrating on finishing the seventh grade at the Doswell Elementary School. Besides, I had never known anyone who was a Jew. In fact, I had never even heard of a Jew in our area. They were mostly in the cities. Mama and Daddy never discussed any of these "European problems" with me and neither were they talked about at school. As I looked forward to summer, little did I know what important things were to happen to me before the end of the year of 1939.

The New York World's Fair

One afternoon in early summer, Mama came out into the yard where I was cutting the grass and said, "Come here, LeRoy, and sit down. I want to talk to you about something."

I thought it strange that she would interrupt her work in the house to come outside to talk to me. I thought it must be something important. Anyway, I was glad for a break. I sat down in one of the lawn chairs next to her.

"We're going to the World's Fair in New York," she said with a broad smile.

"Who, Mama?"

"Just you and I," she continued. "Daddy has to stay here and care for the animals. He wasn't interested anyhow."

I had read something about the World's Fair in "Popular Mechanics" magazine but never had I dreamed of going there myself. I could hardly believe what Mama was telling me.

"How are we gonna get there and where'll we stay?"

"I have it all planned out. You and I will take the train from here down to Norfolk. Then we'll get on a ship that takes all day to sail up to New York. I've written my friend, Mrs. Ethel Davis, in New York and she wants us to stay with her. Doesn't that sound exciting?"

"Boy, it sure does. Will we be on a regular ocean liner?" I was full of questions and still finding it hard to believe this conversation.

"Yes, we'll be in the Atlantic Ocean and go up the coast to New York. The ship will not be as large as the liners that cross the ocean but it will be plenty big."

"When are we going?" My questions continued. This whole idea was mind boggling to me.

"We have reservations about a month from now. I have to get a new suit for you and there are a lot of other things to do. I thought this would be a nice present for you now that you have finished school at Doswell and with such good grades. You know, the fair is supposed to have a lot of exhibits of what the future will be and I know they will be interesting to you." (Mama was thinking about my future and wanted to expose me to things beyond the farm.)

"This sounds wonderful, Mama. I never thought I'd get to do anything like this. Thank you a million times! I can hardly believe it!" I gave Mama a hug, something I hadn't done for a long time.

"We'll talk about it some more but I just wanted you to know what I have been planning. Now you go ahead and finish cutting the grass and I'll go in and start lunch."

As I pushed the lawn mower around the yard, many thoughts were

racing in my head. I had never been to New York; I had never been on
an ocean liner and I certainly had never been to anything as exciting
as the New York World's Fair. My experience with fairs had been the
Virginia State Fair, held in Richmond each August. At that fair, the
exhibits were principally agricultural: cows, pigs, chickens and the
like. They also had lots of home exhibits of flowers, bread, cakes and
pies, needlework, fresh fruit and vegetables. For excitement they had
horse racing one day during the week and motorcycle races another. I
really liked the fast and noisy motorcycle races. Of course, they had an
assortment of sideshows. "Pay a dime and come in and see the bearded
lady and the two-headed dwarf," shouted the barker outside the tent.
But these were nothing like the things I would see at the World's Fair.

Mama bought a whole new outfit for me: double breasted Navy
blue suit, white shirt, tie, white shoes and a snappy white cap. "You'll
need the cap to wear on the ship because we'll be out on deck much of
the time; it's really bright on the ocean," Mama cautioned.

I was sure proud of that outfit. When Mama was out of the room,
I slipped on the Navy blue suit jacket over my old work clothes and put
on the while cap. I faced myself in the mirror and imagined strolling
about the deck on that big ship.

The train trip to Norfolk was interesting. We could see open water
from the train long before we got to our destination. I had never seen
such wide expanses of water. Norfolk is at the junction of the James
River and the Chesapeake Bay. Beyond Norfolk is the Atlantic Ocean.
All of the harbors around Norfolk were crowded with Navy ships:
aircraft carriers, battleships, destroyers and all kinds of smaller ships.
I had never seen ships like these except as pictures in Life Magazine.

We had a beautiful warm day for the trip on the ship up the east
coast to New York. Mama sat on the deck reading and talking to the
other passengers just like she was accustomed to traveling on ships. The
ocean was calm and the water was a deep blue-green color. One deck
allowed access all the way to the bow of the ship. I liked to stand there
with the wind blowing in my face and watch the white foam boiling
away as the ship's prow split the water. Another favorite spot was at the

stern where you could watch the wake of the ship stretching out behind for miles, like a great water highway. I was curious about all parts of the ship and busied myself going from deck to deck and bow to stern. Every once in a while I would stop by to see Mama and report on the latest thing I had discovered. We'd talk a few minutes and then I'd be off on another turn around the deck. I wanted to see every inch of the ship and commit it to memory so I could relive this wonderful trip.

Mrs. Ethel Davis, Mama's friend and our host, had an apartment on the fifth floor of her building. She and Mama had known each other for years. Mama first knew her when they both lived in Maryland. She was very friendly to me and was always asking if I would like some cookies or a soft drink or maybe some ice cream. I had never had so many good things offered to me. Mama never objected; she just smiled whenever I accepted some of the goodies offered by Mrs. Davis. I guess she knew this little extravagance for a few days wouldn't hurt me. Besides all the goodies that Mrs. Davis offered, there was the novelty of the elevator. It was self-operated and I found countless reasons to use it to go down to the street level and back. What fun. I could start and stop at any floor, all the while operating it myself. If someone got on, I would ask what floor they wanted and let them off at that floor. Most times I got a smile, a thank you or a wink. I was operating the elevator just like the man at the Miller and Rhodes Department Store in Richmond. I was having a lot of fun and we hadn't yet gone to the World's Fair.

The New York World's Fair was built on 1200 acres in Flushing Meadow, New York. It had been under construction for a couple years and opened for visitors in 1939. They had exhibits from twenty-three states and fifty-eight countries. Just about every country I had ever heard of was represented except Germany. The theme of the fair was "The World of Tomorrow." The centerpiece of the fair, which could be seen from any place in the park, was the Trylon and the Perisphere. The Trylon was a seven hundred feet tall three sided tower; the Perisphere, adjacent to the Trylon, was a gigantic two hundred foot sphere. These two structures were surrounded by fountains and lighted at night. They were like nothing I had ever seen.

Sailing from Norfolk to New York City with my mother en route to the 1939 World's Fair—the trip of a lifetime for a farm boy.

Businesses were displaying and demonstrating their newest inventions and their ideas of what the world would look like in ten or twenty years. All the work saving devices and leisure products were electrical, of course. These things really interested me. This is where I first saw television in the RCA exhibit. The television screen was about six inches square, black and white, of course. They had a video camera behind and above the television set pointed out to where the viewers were. So I walked up to see the screen and suddenly realized I was looking at an image of myself. It was really strange. Besides television, there were electric washing machines, electric clothes dryers, refrigerators that made their own ice and a myriad of other products that were promised the consumer in the future.

For me, one of the most bizarre exhibits was the one from the Soviet Union. It had lots of red, inside and outside, and huge banners with the hammer and sickle. They had figures of Soviet workers, men and women, that were two and three times life size. Inside were lots of photos and murals and literature proclaiming the "wonderful Soviet communistic society."

One of the attendants approached me and began extolling the virtues of the Russian way of life. Mama took me by the arm and gently headed me toward the door. "Don't you believe a word that man told you," she whispered as we walked out into the bright sunshine. Little did I realize at the time how right she was.

I think the most interesting exhibit was the General Motors "Futurama." This was inside an enormous building and was designed to give a "vision of life in 1960." The part that I enjoyed most was a tram that wound around inside a darkened tunnel with one side open looking out on a model of a futuristic city. The view you got from the tram was as if you were in an airplane flying over this city. Besides the normal streets and tall buildings, there were multi-laned highways winding their way through the city. Sometimes the highways were at ground level and other times they were elevated. These giant roadway ribbons were crowded with hundreds of little streamlined cars and trucks and busses. The effect was a world filled with automobiles, all rushing toward their destinations.

At the time, I thought, "Why would you need highways with ten lanes going in each direction? Certainly there would never be enough cars to fill up such roads."

The New York World's Fair was a wonderful experience for me. It certainly gave me a peek into the future which I never would have had from my vantage point on the farm. The country was just beginning to emerge from the Depression and the Fair was designed to lift the spirits and to give hope that better things lie ahead. I think it did that for the twenty-five million people that attended it in 1939. It was a diversion from the horrible things going on elsewhere in the world.

But, in a way, it was an expression of the isolationism prevalent in our country at the time. The Fair said, "Don't be bothered by all that trouble in Europe; it doesn't concern us. Be happy; good times are coming." I was naive enough at that time just to believe most of that.

The End of Childhood

The fall of 1939 would be my first year at Ashland High School. I looked forward to it with a bit of anxiety. I was comfortable that I could master the academics but just leaving the Doswell School where everything and everybody was familiar gave me a feeling of sadness. As always, Mama encouraged me that this was going to be interesting and fun. Oh well, I had one more week of this nice warm weather I could enjoy before school started. And this Sunday would be fun because Thelma and Raymond and Clara would be coming up from Richmond for a visit.

"Have you heard the news?" Thelma asked Mama and Daddy as she got out of their car.

"What news?" Mama was puzzled.

"The war. Germany invaded Poland on the first of September and then two days later Great Britain and France declared war on Germany. Looks like they've got a real mess over there. Here, we brought you the paper." Thelma displayed the headlines for all to see.

"Can I see the paper?" I asked Mama.

A quick reading of the headlines and the opening paragraphs in the Richmond News Leader told the whole story. Germany had swept into Poland at lightning speed on September 1 with armored vehicles and Stuka dive bombers; Poland met the advancing Germans with their cavalry. The Poles put up a valiant but futile defense. It would be all over in a few weeks. In line with their mutual assistance pact with Poland, the British and French declared war on Germany on September 3, 1939. Another article on the first page said that President Roosevelt emphasized that the United States would remain neutral. To me, this was a distant conflict in Europe; little did I or anyone else in our family realize that it was the beginning of World War II and would affect every one of us for the next six years.

As Mama had predicted, Ashland High was not as formidable as I had feared. I had friends from Doswell that rode on the school bus with me and the classes were interesting. This day was one of those bright warm September days and I was feeling good as I walked into the kitchen from school. Mama was not in the kitchen, where she usually was this time of the day, starting supper.

I put my books down on the corner of the kitchen table and headed through the living room on my way up to my room to change clothes. As I walked down the hall past Mama's room, I saw her sitting over near the far window hunched over with her head in her hands.

"Mama, are you all right?" I asked, walking into the room. She didn't answer. I walked over and put my hand on her shoulder. She was sobbing. I had never before seen her cry. I knew something terrible must have happened.

"Mama, what's the matter? Can you talk to me?"

She continued sobbing with her head buried between her hands. I knew she was embarrassed to have me see her like this. I was scared. Mama was always the strong one. What terrible thing could have happened to make her cry like this?

"Mama, what happened? Please talk to me." I begged.

She wiped her eyes and, without looking up, reached out and grasped my hand.

"Oh, LeRoy,——— I'm so unhappy. I wish I could die." The words struck me like a thunderbolt. My throat was dry and I could hardly speak.

"Don't say that, Mama. Is it something I did?" I stooped down beside her chair and put my arm around her.

"No, no.——- Of course not." I was waiting for some explanation. She was trying to get her sobbing under control. After a minute or so, she wiped her eyes, put on her glasses and turned to look at me. Her eyes were all red from crying and she had the saddest look on her face. We just looked at each other for a moment and then she said, "Bring that chair over and sit by me and I'll talk with you."

I sat down close beside her and she reached out and took my hand. I waited for her explanation. She continued to wipe away the tears and was obviously struggling to decide how to begin to explain. A long time passed and neither of us said anything.

Finally, she spoke very softly, "Your Daddy and I have decided to separate."

"What do you mean, Mama?" I was incredulous.

"You and I will leave the farm." I couldn't believe the words.

"But——why?— Where will we go?"

"I am not sure. Maybe to someplace in Doswell, maybe to Richmond." She wiped her eyes.

"But— when would we go?" My mind was spinning with questions.

"Not for a while——-maybe a few weeks." Her voice was halting and tears welled up in her eyes again. "I can't explain everything to you right now. We'll talk some more another time. Now, you go change your clothes and get on with your chores. I have to start supper."

"Are you going to be all right, Mama?" I asked.

"I'll be all right. I'll just sit here a few minutes. You go now."

There was a sort of strange quietness over the house the next couple weeks. Activities proceeded as usual, but conversations between all of us were matter of fact. Several times after I went up to bed I heard quiet conversations between Mama and Daddy, but I couldn't hear what they were saying. I lay in my bed for a long time thinking, *Why? What could it be? I never heard any quarrelling between them. They had slept in separate bedrooms for as long as I could remember. But that didn't mean anything. Maybe there was something I had done and Mama just didn't want to tell me.* I worried about all the possibilities I could think of. Finally, I drifted off into a restless sleep.

On Saturday morning, Mama said, "LeRoy, I want you to drive me out to Doswell. I have some things to get." I backed the car out of the garage and waited for her. Mama came out of the house and walked slowly to the car. She got in, closed the door and just sat quietly for a minute.

Finally, as if returning from some deep thought, she said, "Well, let's go."

She was obviously preoccupied and said little. Usually we chatted as we drove along the dirt road toward Doswell, not today. She asked to stop at Campbell's General Store. After she had bought a few groceries, she said we should drive out to Highway #1 that she wanted to look at a place.

"There's a house for rent up behind where the old blacksmith shop used to be. We ought to have a look at it."

"Is that where we might live when we leave the farm, Mama," I inquired as we turned on to the highway.

"Well, maybe. We'll see."

The house was only about a mile from Doswell. As we pulled into the yard, Mama said, "Just park here and come in with me."

The owner of the house met us at the door and offered to show us about. It was small. It seemed almost like a cottage compared to our old farmhouse. It had two bedrooms, a kitchen and a living room and, of course, a bathroom. I could see Mama was not overly impressed. Even thinking about living here as opposed to our home on the farm made me sad. I loved that little alcove up on the second floor that was my bedroom. The thought that I was going to leave the farm pushed into my mind. As much as I could, I had kept it sort of in an abstract form in my mind. Was this really where we might end up living?

While we were alone in one of the bedrooms, Mama whispered, "LeRoy, why don't you wait in the car while I speak to the owner a few minutes."

It was a beautiful September day, but it didn't lighten my spirits any. I hoped Mama didn't decide to rent this place; it was depressing to me. It was not more than a hundred feet off the highway and the traffic, especially the trucks, made a horrendous noise as they sped by.

Mama came out to the car and got in without saying a word. I waited for her to tell me what she had decided. After an awkward silence, I asked, "Are we going to live here, Mama?"

"No. It's not suitable and we don't have that much money. Start the car; we're going home."

"Good. I didn't like it anyway."

As we drove toward home, I began to wonder what other possibilities there were. "Where are we going to live, Mama?"

"I don't know just yet. I've written Uncle Page in Richmond and asked if he has any places where we might stay. You know he owns several houses." Mama sounded very tired and discouraged. Uncle Page was her brother and a dentist who did a little real estate on the side.

Mama got a letter from Uncle Page the next week. She didn't tell me the contents but at breakfast on Saturday she announced in a matter of fact tone, "Ira, LeRoy and I are driving down to Richmond today to see Page and Hettie. We'll be back tonight." Hettie, Aunt Hettie to me, was Mama's old maid sister who lived with her bachelor brother, Page. I looked across the table to see Daddy's reaction but there was none. Perhaps Mama and Daddy had already discussed the possibility of our moving to Richmond. It was strange. I knew this might signal the start of a new life for Mama and me but there was no discussion at all.

"LeRoy, you go and get dressed and then see that the car is clean inside. We'll leave in an hour or so," Mama said as she cleared the breakfast dishes from the table.

Once on the road out to Doswell, I couldn't contain my curiosity any longer, "What did Uncle Page say? Does he have a house where we might live?"

"Well, he said he had two houses: a small one down on the property where he and Hettie live and another one on Marshall Street in Richmond. I'm to telephone him when we get outside of Richmond and he said he would meet us at the house on Marshall Street. It's in Church Hill. I have the number written down here; it's 3415 East Marshall Street. You know, LeRoy, it's interesting. That would be 34th Street and Marshall. Did I ever tell you that my home where I grew up was also in that part of Richmond? We lived on 29th Street near Marshall. Oh, but that was a long time ago."

We drove on down Highway 1 toward Richmond with little conversation. I was trying to concentrate on driving but I kept thinking of what lay ahead. I had so many questions but I also knew Mama didn't have all the answers. I kept thinking of my life on the farm and now it was all ending. I couldn't imagine what it would be like to live in the city. I knew Mama was worrying about all these things and many more and that was why she was so quiet.

When we reached the outskirts of Richmond, Mama pointed to a gas station ahead and said, "Pull in over there and I'll call Page while we get some gas."

Mama telephoned Uncle Page and then we drove into the city of

Richmond turning east on Broad Street. Broad Street was the main shopping street and where the big department stores were, Thalheimers and Miller Rhodes. We passed through the main business district and continued on east toward the area called Church Hill. This was an older residential part of Richmond that dated back to the Civil War.

"Oh, look to your right, LeRoy. That's old St. John's Episcopal Church where I attended when I was growing up and where your daddy and I were married," Mama said.

"Will we go to that church if we move to Richmond?" I asked.

"Yes, if we end up living over here on Church Hill," Mama answered. "St. John's is where Patrick Henry made that famous speech before the Revolutionary War. That's where he said, 'Give me liberty or give me death.' You must have studied that in history at school."

A few blocks farther on Mama said, " See that house over there with the porch; that's where I grew up." Though she said nothing more, I could tell she was pleased to be in the neighborhood where she had lived as a girl.

"Turn here on 34th Street and go one block and that should be Marshall Street," Mama directed. "The house number is 3415."

I parked the car in front of 3415 and Mama and I got out. Uncle Page was already there and he came forward to greet us, "Well, you made it all right. Hello, Sallie. LeRoy, you've grown some more since I saw you last. Come on, let's go in and have a look."

Though similar to the other houses on the block, 3415 was not really a row house. It had a narrow alley about three feet wide on each side separating it from the adjoining houses. A few stone steps in front led up to a small porch and the front door. We entered into a hall with stairs that led to the second floor. On our left downstairs were three rooms. First, a living room in front that faced on the porch and looked out on the street. Next was another room, probably meant as a dining room, and in back was the kitchen. Uncle Page said the house had been rented until a month ago. What struck me immediately was all the trash left in the house: newspaper, cardboard boxes and even an open can of beans on the kitchen sink. I could see Mama didn't like all the trash.

"Well, it'll take a little cleaning," said Uncle Page, casually. "Renters are like that. They seem to think someone else should clean up their mess when they leave. Let's have a look upstairs."

We climbed the stairs and found a similar arrangement of rooms upstairs. There were the three rooms in line just as there were downstairs. These were the bedrooms. In addition, there was a small room right at the head of the stairs, maybe meant as a walk-in closet. A bathroom was accessible from the hall. Off the bedroom in the back was a small room that had once been an upstairs porch. It looked just big enough for a single bed and a small dresser. It had a torn mattress in it indicating it had been used as a bedroom. The general condition upstairs was similar to the downstairs: dirty, but with a little less trash.

Mama walked back and forth through the upstairs rooms without saying anything. I knew she must be trying to figure out how our furniture would fit and how we could fix up this house and make it livable. Obviously there was plenty of room for just the two of us.

While we were upstairs, I heard a rumble noise coming from the street in front of the house. "What was that?" I asked Mama and Uncle Page.

"Oh, that's just the streetcar. Didn't you notice the tracks when you drove up," said Uncle Page. "You'll get used to it after you live here awhile. Mighty convenient. You can catch it right across the street and it'll take you right uptown."

I wondered if I'd ever get used to that noise of the streetcar. It sure was strange compared to the quiet of the farm. I was just beginning to realize all the things that would be different living in the city compared to the farm.

"Come on downstairs and I'll show you the back yard," said Uncle Page. "The renters never did anything with it, but you could plant grass and fix it up. There's room for you to have some flowers, Sallie."

The backyard was filled with knee-high weeds all turned brown this time of the year. Numerous tin cans and paper trash littered the yard. In the far corner was a small shack.

"That's your coal house," said Uncle Page. "The house has hot water heat. You saw the radiators in all the rooms. The furnace was that big stove right in the kitchen. Keeps the kitchen nice and warm."

As we drove through Richmond on our way back to the farm, Mama asked, "What did you think of the house?" I could tell by the way she asked me that she had already decided that we would move there.

"It's sure got enough room for the two of us. Boy, what a lot of trash and dirt to clean up."

"Yes, it's awful how some people leave a place when they move out. I expect they were pretty messy and dirty when they lived there. But we can clean it up," Mama said. Then she continued, "Page says we'll only have to pay the utilities; he's letting us stay there 'rent free'. We can rent out one or two of the upstairs rooms and that will help to cover some of our expenses."

"I can get a part time job or deliver papers or something while I go to school," I offered.

"Yes, that's possible but I don't want you to do anything that interferes with your schooling. That's the most important thing for you just now. I think we can make do. We would be close to Janice and her family and also to Aunt Hettie and Uncle Page. I understand you would go to John Marshall High School which is a big school and much better than Ashland High. We would be close to St. John's Episcopal Church. I would enjoy going there again." Mama was cataloging all the advantages of moving to 3415 East Marshall Street.

"When would we leave the farm and move?" I asked.

"I'll arrange for a truck to take our furniture down to Richmond. I think we could pack up in a week. Page said we could stay with him until we get the place cleaned up and our furniture gets delivered."

"What furniture will we take, Mama?" I asked.

" I plan to take that round oak table in the kitchen, the small cherry table I use as a desk and that chair we've had since our wedding. Of course, we'll have to take our bedroom furniture and some chairs, too. Oh, I'd like to take my favorite rocking chair. I'll have to look around and decide on other things. I want to leave your Daddy adequate furnishings so he is comfortable."

Mama was clearly anxious to move as quickly as possible and she had worked out the plan already. Then it was settled. We were leaving the farm and moving to Richmond. I pondered on these thoughts as we drove on to the farm.

During the next week, Mama and I finished our packing and the truck was coming today, Saturday, to load up what furniture we were taking to Richmond. I told Mama I wanted a little time to look around the farm before we left. I took my bicycle and rode down the hill beside the barn where we had had such fun years ago playing with our sleds in the snow. At the bottom of the hill was the pasture where Emil Brenckman had landed the Army biplane when I was a little kid. That memory was so vivid in my mind that I felt it was just a day or so ago. I pedaled onto the flats where we had grown our watermelons, cantaloupes and strawberries. Now that it was October, nothing remained but the dried vines. A little farther on along the road I passed the sand pit where Daddy and I had hauled many a wagonload of sand for repairing our road going toward Doswell. Just past the sandpit on my right was that big old cedar tree which marked one boundary of the farm. It was the favorite place for that old owl that I used to hear as I lay in my upstairs bed on summer nights. But he was not in his usual roosting spot on that big limb.

I parked my bicycle in the edge of the woods and took the path down toward the river. The river was low because we had not had much rain. Standing on the high bank looking down at the "swimming hole," I remembered the fun we had had in those lazy days of summer. How refreshing it had been to dive into that cool water after a long day of hauling hay or bagging wheat at the threshing machine! Swimming in the North Anna River was such an important part of our summertime recreation. There was the "grand adventure" when Gretchen, Roger and I built that little boat that leaked so badly that we had to bail it out every few minutes so one of us could ride in it. And there was the time my little submarine that I had made was swept away by the current. As I turned and headed back up the path, memories flooded my mind of the good times we spent at the river. Just before I came out of the woods, I remembered the "old Indian spring" and wondered if I could still find it. Sure enough, it was the same, a steady stream of cool sweet water flowing out of a mossy bank into a hollowed-out stone shaped like a basin. I knelt down beside the spring and scooped up water with my hands and had a good drink. The water tasted fresh and cold, just as it always had.

Instead of going directly back to the house, I wandered through our fruit orchard and came out on the field to the north of our farmhouse. A turkey buzzard was lazily circling high above the field, riding the thermals. All was quiet; it was so peaceful. Not likely would I see sights like this again when we moved to the city. I would miss seeing the geese flying south this year, too. They were always an exciting sight, flying in a great chevron formation and honking as they went. These were the fields where we had grown our corn and hauled hay into the barn. The fall season always made me a little sad because the crops had completed their life cycle and all about were just the dead remnants. Only the dried corn stubble remained in the fields.

Daddy was loading boxes into the trunk of our car as I walked up to the farmhouse. I could see the car was fully loaded. He turned and walked toward me.

"Now, LeRoy, you take care of your mother. You hear?" He said, giving me a firm handshake.

I suddenly realized this was goodbye. My throat felt dry and tears welled up as I answered in a half-whisper, "OK." I wanted to say more but I couldn't think what to say.

With no more conversation, Daddy turned and walked toward the barn. No final goodbye, this was it. When Daddy walked away, that was the last I saw of him – ever.

I felt a strange sadness because I knew I was leaving the life on the farm for an entirely new life in the city. I had spent my entire life of fourteen years on the farm. Despite the hard work, I loved the farm. I loved the open fields, the smell of fresh cut hay in the spring and waking up to the crowing of a rooster in the early morning. And a hundred other things. But I also realized that moving to the city offered lots of advantages: a better high school, new friends, the chance to earn some money in a part-time job and many others. Mama had said that it was natural to be sad about leaving the farm but that I was growing up now and had to prepare for my future.

I knew she was right.

THE END

Appendix

The Family Line of LeRoy E. Day[2]

(John, James, Luther, Rufus King,
Latimer, Ira, LeRoy)

Day Family Bibles

James Day, who with his descendents is the subject of this Appendix, was the first of his family to keep records. There are references in legal documents of a Family Bible, long since lost.

In 1869, John Fletcher Boyer, a son-in-law of James' son, Jackson, and a grandson of James' daughter, Elizabeth Day Boyer, made a copy of the information. This copy became the source of lists which circulated widely among the family, and this copy, still owned by Susan E. Boyer, is the only record which exists of our earliest Day ancestors.

This list includes James Day and the many children of his several marriages, with their dates of birth. Also listed were James' parents, John Day and his wife, Sarah, born in 1720 and 1727, respectively.

Who John's parents or grandparents were is simply not known at this time. The efforts of descendents pursuing their curiosity and checking old records for any trace of those who came before John have recently been complemented by the efforts of a professional genealogist, without success. In so far as proofs are concerned, John Day is as far back as anyone can go. But there were Days before John, and among them would be his ancestors.

Day Beginnings

There is much agreement that the first Days lived in Wales and that the family is of Celtic origin. One source of family names is a place. In Wales there is a small river called Dee, and the river's name could have become attached to the people who lived on its banks. Later with migration and changes of language, Dee became Daye and then Day.

"In a book of Heraldry containing the arms of William Day, B.D., Provost of Eaton College and Dean of Windsor, confirmed by William Flower on October 21, 1582 in the twenty fourth year of Queen Elizabeth's reign, he is said to have descended from the Dean of Wales, viz., being the youngest son of Richard Day, who was the son of Nicholas Day the son of John Dee"[3]

Another source of names consists of adjectives of colors and qualities. The name Day could be derived from words meaning either 'good' (Celtic Deag, Gaelic Dagh, Welsh Dai) or 'dark' (Welsh Du, referring to complexion or hair, Gaelic Dhu, dark color, black, Anglo-Saxon Deah, dark, obscure)[4]

It is likely that in these and other fashions several unrelated families each adopted the name Day. It is not an exceptionally uncommon name. When the colonies were first settled, numbers of Days were among the settlers of each.

Refugees, Immigrants, Servants

The origins of English settlement in Maryland date to 1637, and within fifty years of that date over two dozen persons named Day had arrived. The first person named Day to arrive in Maryland did not come directly by sea, but was a refugee from religious persecution in Virginia. Richard Day, a Dissenter, arrived in Providence (now called Anne Arundel County) in 1649. In 1642, Richard Bennett, member of an English trading company, had brought to Virginia "members of an Independent Church in England, who sought a more favorable field for building up their church."[5] They settled on the Elizabeth River in Nasemond County, Virginia, but ran into trouble with the Established Church of England. In 1649 several of these settlers, including Richard Day, "were presented to ye board by the sheriff, for seditious sectuaries for not repairing to their church, and for refusing to hear common prayer."[6] Given a year to repent, they left Virginia instead, for lands along the Severn and Patuxent which they would call Providence.

Other Days came by sea from England. Those who were more well off were termed 'Immigrants' meaning that they were able to pay their own way and sometimes that of others, thereby receiving grants of land for each person's passage paid. A John Day who arrived in Anne Arundel County in 1652 was such an Immigrant,[7]as were Robert Day of Calvert County and George Day of St. Mary's. Robert received a grant of land called "The Angle" in 1659[8] and was listed as a resident of Leonard Creek on the Patuxent River when he witnessed a will in 1679.[9] George was among the 1000 earliest settlers with land surveys recorded in Lord Baltimore's rent rolls. His land, called 'Burwastcott,' was surveyed May 5, 1665.[10]

In addition to the immigrants who paid their own way across the Atlantic, other Day settlers were 'transported' as indentured servants, agreeing to virtual slavery for seven years in exchange for passage. "Immediately after he signed the contract, an indenture often found himself imprisoned...When the boats docked, the servants were assembled on deck so planters could interview them and feel their muscles. The servants were then auctioned off to the highest bidder... The term of indenture was short and many masters wanted to be sure they got their money's worth. In the early years they drove their servants so hard that the back-breaking regime combined with crude living conditions caused over 50 per cent of the servants to die."[11] Yet after service was over they were the equal of any, and in 1637 fifteen former indentured servants had seats in the first Maryland Assembly.[12]

A Nicholas Day, an indentured servant transported from England in 1658[13] founded a large family on the Gunpowder River north of Baltimore, whose descendents later migrated to North Carolina and Tennessee. An Edward Day, transported in 1671,[14] founded a family on the Eastern Shore and witnessed a will in Talbot County in 1686.[15]

Among the Days who lived in St. Mary's, one helped contribute a first to American life. On September 22, 1656, Dorothy Day sat on a jury in the town of St. Mary's to determine if Judith Catchpole was guilty of infanticide. This is the first recorded instance of women jurors in the New World.[16]

Family of John Day, father of James

John Day was born in 1720. He was 40 and his wife 37 when their eldest child was born. In that time, long before the advent of birth control, children followed quickly after marriage, and so, even in the absence of any marriage records, it may be surmised that John Day married around 1759, when he was 39. According to the Family Bible, John and Sarah Day had four children. Mary was born December 28, 1760; James, September 8, 1762; Elizabeth, November 10, 1764, and John, October 17, 1766.

John Day died while his family was still young. On October 1, 1772, at the age of 52, he died, as he had lived, under the flag of England. Sarah lived another 21 years, long enough to witness the Revolution and the birth of a new nation, before her own death November 5, 1793.

Family of James Day

On the day of his birth Maryland was a proprietary colony of England, whose King was George III. The French and Indian War had yet to conclude its waning days. Its end, when James was one year old, brought an outpouring of patriotic sentiment for King George. Not until twelve years more had passed would growing unhappiness occasion talk of separation from England.[17]

When James was almost 13, a British attempt to regain Massachusetts led to the first fighting of the Revolution at Lexington and Concord.[18] When James was 14, the colonies, after a year of war, declared their independence.

Whatever led up to it, "in the spring of the year 1778," (when he was about 15 ½ years old), James Day "entered the Service as a volunteer soldier in the Company commanded by John H. Nichols."[19] "He volunteered to serve for nine months…He was stationed in George Town for some time and was then ordered to Annapolis…Upon arriving at Bladensburgh the order was countermanded and he was ordered … to Frederick Town … to guard the Prisoners of War who were at the old Barracks in Frederick…" (17) Service in the war entitled James Day to receive a pension in later life of $30 per year.

In 1779, war service completed and aged 16, James Day again disappears from view for five years. During that period the war itself was concluded; after Cornwallis' surrender at Yorktown in October 1781, little remained but long months of diplomacy, until the Treaty of Paris was signed February 3, 1783 and the last British troops left New York November 25, 1783.[20]

In that period there must have occurred the hard work required for getting a start in adult responsibility, as well as the courtship of young Cassandra Beall, age16,whom James Day, now 21, married on June 8,1784.[21] Cassandra was the daughter of Clement Beall, member of a very well documented Maryland family.

The first child of James and Cassandra was named Aquila. In 1789, four years after Aquila's birth, a second child was born whom they named Christie. The Census of the following year recorded the four of them, and five slaves, located in the First District of Montgomery County. They probably lived in the Seneca-Darnestown area because in the 1790 Census he is listed next to Charles Gassaway, who was a large landowner in the Seneca area between the Potomac River and Darnestown. It is not known when James Day became a slave owner; no records of purchase have been located. The Census listing, however, that by 1790, at the age of 28, James Day had already begun to gather about him the prosperity of family and property he would later have.

Soon, however, came a winter bleak with deaths. In November of 1793, James' mother died at the age of 66. Then four days after the turn of the year, Cassandra died. Very shortly after, Cassandra's father died as well. James Day, at 31, was left with a nine year old son, daughters aged five and two, and his slaves.

After Cassandra died, James married Sallie Warfield on November 7, 1795. She bore him eight children. On December 18, 1821, his wife Sallie died. By this time the last of his slaves may well have been gone; left at home with James Day, aged 59, were children aged 7, 12, 14, 16, and 18 to help him keep the household together.

Almost two years later, on September 21, 1823, soon after his 61st birthday, James Day married for the third time. He married Sarah Mark, 24 years old, younger than his five oldest children. James and his wife, Sarah, had 7 children. All in all, James Day had 18 children with his three wives.

Children of James Day and Cassandra Beall

1. Aquila, born October 4, 1785
2. Christie, born November 7, 1789
3. Matilda, born November 23, 1792

Children of James Day and Sallie Warfield.

1. Elizabeth, born September 22, 1796
2. Urban, born December 1, 1798
3. Mary Polly, born February 24, 1801
4. Luther, born August 26, 1803
5. Lorenzo, born August 10, 1805
6. Jefferson, born November 4, 1807
7. Hester Ann, bornNovember1809
8. Sarah Ann, born March 22, 1814

Children of James Day and Sarah Mark

1. Caroline, born July 3, 1824
2. Amanda Malvina, born October 28, 1825 3. Arminus, born July 30, 1827
3. James Wilkerson, born July 30, 1827
4. Jackson, born September 27, 1830
5. Madison Livingston, born April 11, 1834
6. Franklin B, born November 10, 1836

James Day was a Methodist all of his life. At the time of James Day, the Methodists firmly objected to slaveholding. Records indicate that he released his slaves over a period of time and by December 21, 1821, when his wife Sallie died, all of his slaves were gone. Besides practicing his religion, he became a preacher and traveled to various churches in his area. In addition to acting as a preacher, he took the lead in establishing the Bethesda Chapel in Browningsville, Maryland. Later, together with others, they built a Methodist Protestant Church near Kemptown, close to where the present Providence Methodist Protestant Church now stands. The latter church is where my mother and father first met.

The Family of Luther Day

Luther Day was born August 26, 1803, the fourth child of James Day and Sallie Warfield. On January 18, 1825 he married Harriet Ann King, whose father owned a large farm in a nearby area still known as King's Valley. Soon two children joined the family, but Luther was not to see his children grow up; three years after the marriage, in 1828, when he was 25, Luther Day died. A memorial stone was erected to him when the cemetery at the Providence Church in Kemptown was created.

His two children were:

1. Elizabeth M, born in 1826
2. Rufus King, born May 18, 1827

Family of Rufus King Day

Rufus King was a farmer in Frederick County, 3 miles from Browningsville. He married Ann Priscilla Brandenburg, October 23, 1849. He was described as follows: *Mr. Day is a self-reliant man, who began life without means, even without the advantage of a good education, and who has secured a competency by a life of uniform industry and determination.* In addition to his farming, he sold fertilizer for 30 years and also was a Judge of elections for two years. He is buried in the Bethesda Chapel Cemetery, Browningsville. His children were:

1. Titus Granville, born September 16, 1850
2. Latimer W., born 1852
3. Addison S., born 1856
4. Altona B., born October 22, 1857
5. Preston C., born October 21, 1859
6. Harriet Emma, born 1863
7. James Start, born 1865
8. Laura Arvila, born July 11, 1867
9. Langdon Storrs, born 1871
10. Nora May, born August 14, 1875

Family of Latimer W. Day

Latimer Day was the second son of Rufus King Day. He was a prosperous tobacco farmer near Kemptown, Maryland. He married Venia W. Browning on November 12, 1878. She was 21 years old. They had three children:

1. Venia Wynonia
2. Ira Eugene, born November 28, 1879
3. Melissa B, born 1883

Family of Ira Day

Ira Day married Sallie Caskie Lester in Richmond, Virginia, on December 11, 1902.

Sallie Lester was born December 9, 1881, in Richmond, Virginia. They lived on Latimer Day's farm for 10 years where Ira continued to help his father produce tobacco. In 1913 they moved to a farm at Doswell, Virginia. They divorced on March 17, 1947. Ira died April 8, 1955 and is buried at the Calvary Christian Church, near Ashland, Virginia. Sallie died September 19, 1963 and is buried at Fork Church, Doswell, Virginia. They had eight children.

1. Janice Louise, born June 5, 1904, died May 6, 1997
2. Claude Randolph, born October 21, 1906, died Oct 23, 1973
3. Thelma Lester, born August 27, 1910, died April 13, 1997
4. Clara Lavinia, born March 1, 1913, died December 9, 2000
5. Robert Adrian, born November 4, 1915, died Feb 18, 2004
6. Margaret Antonia, born June 21, 1918, died Feb 24, 1998
7. Emil Rodney, born August 12, 1921
8. LeRoy Edward, born January 2, 1925

Family of LeRoy Day

LeRoy Day spent his childhood on the Day farm near Doswell, Virginia, and moved to Richmond, Virginia, with his mother when his parents separated. After high school in Richmond, he joined the U. S. Navy in June 1943, was trained at Tulane University, New Orleans, and at Georgia Tech, Atlanta, Georgia. He graduated from Georgia Tech as an Aeronautical Engineer and received his commission as Ensign, U. S. Navy, in June, 1946. He served two years in the Navy at the Naval Missile Test Center, Pt. Mugu, California. He continued as an engineer at the Naval Missile Test Center until the spring of 1962 when he joined the manned space program at the National Aeronautics and

Space Agency (NASA) Headquarters, Washington, D.C. At NASA he was involved in the management of three of the manned programs: Gemini, Apollo and Space Shuttle. He also holds advanced degrees from University of California, Los Angeles, and the Massachusetts Institute of Technology, Cambridge, Massachusetts..

LeRoy Day married Mary Elizabeth Hornbuckle on May 18, 1947 at Capitol Avenue Baptist Church, Atlanta, Georgia. Mary was born 3 September, 1925. They have three children:

1. David Franklin, born January 13, 1949
2. Jean Shirley, born August 3, 1951
3. Michael Phillip, born 15 May 1957

Descendents of LeRoy E. Day

1. David Franklin Day was born in Oxnard, California. He is an attorney in business and international law and a lecturer for the University of Hawaii. He lives in Honolulu, Hawaii. He married (1) Ingrid Korth in 1970 in Hawaii. She was born December 17, 1949 in Brynmawr, Pennsylvania. They were divorced in 1982. He married (2) Ronda Ching in 1991 in Hawaii. She was born March 27, 1959 in Honolulu, Hawaii.
   1a. Child of David Day and Ingrid Korth is: Stefan Christopher Day, born 27 December, 1980 in Oakland, CA
   1b. Child of David Day and Ronda Ching is: Lauren Wei Jeyan Day, born November 20, 1994 in Honolulu, Hawaii
2. Jean Shirley Day was born August 3, 1951 in Oxnard, California. She is an Interior Decorator in Belmont, California. She married Allen Cary in Washington, DC on July 27, 1974. He was born May 15, 1950
3. Michael Phillip Day was born May 15, 1957 in Oxnard,

California. He is a pilot and an aircraft mechanic, living in Bellingham, Washington. He married (1) Jean Green on August 27, 1984 in Kauai, Hawaii. They were divorced in 2002. He married (2) Margaret "Peg" Power on September 4, 2003, in Bellingham, Washington. Margaret was born April 11, 1950.

Epilogue

City Life

Life in the city of Richmond was sure different from life on the farm. Although Uncle Page had generously let us use the house on Marshall Street without any rent, we still had to pay all utilities, our food, any new clothes, doctor bills, medicine and whatever school expenses I had. The first thing Mama did was to advertise for a roomer. Within a couple weeks she had rented the two front upstairs rooms to Mrs. Adkins. To help out, I worked at various odd jobs while I went to John Marshall High School. This was our income. Mama was a good money manager and we made it all right although there were few luxuries.

John Marshall was a two thousand student school with a cadet corp, a football team, an orchestra, a drama club and more. The school building was enormous—three floors plus a basement. It had a large auditorium and all the facilities and equipment for a first class high school, which it was. John Marshall High was located in downtown Richmond. The other large high school, Thomas Jefferson, was located in the west end of the city. At first, I was a little bit overwhelmed, but I quickly fell into the routine and found the studies interesting but hard. The teachers were excellent. Once the war started, all parties and proms were canceled. Science and math classes were strengthened. The girls were involved in various Red Cross activities. The girls were also enrolled in the Victory Corp which emphasized physical training; boys could join the cadet corp. The Victory Corp was organized into companies and platoons and they learned how to march in formation. Sometimes our Victory Corp marched in city parades along with soldiers and sailors. Even with all this activity, we still had time for fun. But it was certainly different from the much smaller Ashland High!

I took a variety of part time jobs. One of the first ones I had was delivering groceries on a bicycle. This was fairly typical in those days. People would call in their order, it would be filled and I would load it in the big basket on the bicycle and ride off to deliver it. When there were no deliveries, I stocked the shelves with dry goods. The pay wasn't much; I received $1.25 for Friday after school until seven o'clock and then all day on Saturday. Of course, prices were much lower at that time. Bread cost 9 cents a loaf; coffee was 30 cents a pound; sugar, 6 cents a pound; a copy of Life magazine was 10 cents and a movie ticket for a double feature was only 25 cents. Salaries were low, too. A college graduate started at about $1200 a year; a public school teacher made $1500; and someone in the building trades might make $1600 a year.

From the "groceries delivery job," I moved to a catering service run by a woman just a couple blocks from our house. Mrs. Gayle made ham and chicken sandwiches and chicken salad every morning for delivery to delicatessen shops around the city's industrial areas. I prepared sandwiches every morning from five thirty to seven and then came home for breakfast before I went off to school. One summer I worked at Baker's Shoes on Broad Street. Fitting and selling shoes to women who had trouble making a selection was quite an experience. Often a woman would tell you her shoe size but invariably that size was too tight and I had to convince her that she really needed the next larger size. I guess the women were sensitive about their shoe size and hated to admit that their feet were really bigger than they imagined.

In my junior year of high school I was hired as a stock boy by Thalheimers, one of the two big department stores in Richmond. I worked in the warehouse and filled orders for the men's clothing department after school and on Saturdays. Sometimes if there was a lot of business on Saturday, I would be allowed to come over to the main store and sell shirts, neckties, underwear, socks and other items to the customers. That was interesting and I learned a lot about men's clothing. Mr. Brent was the buyer of that men's department and he was a strict boss. Of course, I had to wear a coat and tie and look just like the other salesman. When shipments of new merchandise arrived, we had to work after the store closed to stock the new items. Whenever we got a shipment of men's shirts that were "seconds," I was able to look them over and sometimes buy a really nice brand of shirt at a big discount. It may have been graded as a "second" just because it had some minor flaw like poor stitching on the tail of the shirt which didn't even show. I had some of the nicest shirts of any high school boy around.

I remember well that fateful Sunday, December 7, 1941, when the Japanese attacked Pearl Harbor in Hawaii. I was a sixteen year old high schooler. My mother and I had just returned from church and we were having our lunch and listening to the news on our Philco radio. Of course, we didn't know the full extent of casualties and damage at Pearl Harbor but we had a terrible feeling that that day would mark the beginning of total involvement of the United States in World War II. The next day President Roosevelt declared war on Germany and Japan.

His speech was relayed to all of the classrooms at school. I remember him saying, "Yesterday, December 7, 1941—a date which will live in infamy—the United States of America was suddenly and deliberately attacked. With confidence in our armed forces, with the unbounding determination of our people, we will gain the inevitable triumph, so help us God." From that day on, everyone became totally committed to the war, in one way or another.

Beginning in the summer of 1942, between my junior and senior years of high school, I worked in the newly formed Military Uniform Department of Thalheimers. Large numbers of young men were graduating and being commissioned as Second Lieutenants in the Army from the Officers Candidate School at nearby Camp Lee, Virginia. A new class graduated about every month and we were kept busy fitting them out with their new officer's uniforms. Many of the men weren't much older than I and their experiences in training were of great interest to me. To accommodate the servicemen, our department stayed open until 10 PM weeknights and Saturdays and also on Sunday afternoons. I continued working this schedule during my senior year. It was ideal for me. I could put in about twenty hours per week while I was going to school. The rent from the rooms upstairs and my part time jobs provided enough money to cover our expenses.

Navy Life

By December 1942 the war was raging in both Europe and the Pacific. At this time, President Roosevelt announced that the draft-eligible age was lowered from twenty to eighteen years. That announcement caught my attention because my eighteenth birthday was only weeks away on January 2, 1943. I had six months more of my senior year in high school. About that same time the US Navy and the Army announced an Officers College Training Program. I was very interested because I knew it was my only chance to go to college. My grades were good; I was in the National Honor Society but we didn't have the money for college. Even though I hadn't taken a lot of college preparatory courses, I thought I could qualify. This was a once in a lifetime chance for me. If I could pass all the requirements, I would be the only one in our family to go to college. Based on a recommendation from my high school principal, Mr. Harwood, I indicated a preference for the Navy when I took the qualifying test in early April. The test was given on the same day throughout the entire nation to over 300, 000 young men. After I was notified that I had passed the test, I went for a physical exam and an interview. I remember standing in line with dozens of other young men, all of us naked to our undershorts. I was tall and very lean, bordering on skinny, and many of the others looked to be healthy athletic types. I began to wonder if I could pass the physical. At the time, I was six feet two and a half inches and weighed only 147 pounds. Unknown to me, the Navy liked their sailors to be lean. To my relief, I passed both the physical and the interview.

In November 1943, along with over nine hundred other trainees, I received orders to report to the Navy V-12 Unit at Tulane University, New Orleans. Eight hundred and fifty of us were housed in the gymnasium; the rest were quartered in fraternity houses. We were all apprentice seaman, the lowest rank in the Navy with a pay of fifty dollars per month. The routine was a combination of "boot camp" and academics. We learned to march, run obstacle courses, survive in the water under simulated "abandon ship" drills and much more while attending classes five and half days a week. We attended classes for twelve months a year with two-week breaks between semesters. Besides our regular college academic courses, we also studied Naval History, Naval Protocol and other Navy related courses; all were designed to make us into an "officer and a gentleman." The accelerated pace of the V-12 program allowed us to complete the regular four year requirements in two years and eight months.

Because of my strong interest in airplanes, I wanted very much to be an aeronautical engineer. Whenever there was an opportunity, I indicated to the Navy that I would like to transfer to Georgia Tech and study aeronautical engineering. When I finished my freshman year at Tulane, I was surprised to learn that the Navy was transferring me to Georgia Tech, Atlanta, for study in the School of Aeronautics. I could hardly believe my good fortune. While I was in Atlanta, I met and fell in love with a wonderful girl, Mary Hornbuckle. We met at a YMCA dance for servicemen. It may not have been love at first sight but it was close to it! We dated the five months until I got my degree at Georgia Tech, was commissioned an Ensign and was assigned duty in California. Although I had not yet asked her to marry me, I knew I wanted this woman to be a permanent part of my life.

I completed my studies at Georgia Tech in June 1946 with a Bachelor's Degree in Aeronautical Engineering and a commission of Ensign in the US Navy Reserve. I had hoped to be assigned to an aircraft carrier but World War II had been over nearly a year and the Navy was reducing the number of officers in the fleet. In fact, the Navy gave us a choice of active duty or a return to civilian life. After spending all that time learning to be "an officer and a gentleman," I chose active duty. Along with about a dozen of my classmates, the Navy ordered us to the Pilotless Aircraft Unit, Mojave, California. After a short stay at Mojave, we were transferred to the newly established Naval Missile Test Center at Point Mugu, California, on the coast about fifty miles north of Los Angeles. This location had been selected because it provided an excellent range over the Pacific Ocean for the test of guided missiles. I was assigned to the Guidance Laboratory where I had a chance to use my engineering on various projects involving aerodynamics and flight controls. After a year at Pt. Mugu, I returned to Atlanta and married that girl that had caught my eye at the YMCA dance. I was still stationed at Pt. Mugu and Mary and I returned to California to take up married life in the Navy.

Back to Civilian Life

A year after Mary and I were married, I resigned from active duty and continued in the Inactive Naval Reserve while I worked as a civilian engineer for the Naval Missile Test Center. During this time I had the privilege of working with several of the German scientists who were assigned to our base. After World War II a number of German scientists were brought to the US. Twelve came to our base; some went to the Air Force at Wright Field and a large number who had worked on the V-2 missile with Werner Von Braun were sent to the Army at Fort Bliss, Texas. I was promoted to several positions in the Guidance Lab and finally made Head, Guidance Lab in mid-1950. At that time I was one of the youngest division heads on the base. When I became Division Head, we had about eighty personnel in branches that were involved in infrared and radar guidance, simulation, flight controls, aerodynamics, missile warhead lethality and systems analysis.

By this time Mary and I had two children, David and Jean, and a home in Camarillo (about ten miles inland from Pt. Mugu). Although we had been married in Mary's Baptist church in Atlanta, we found an Episcopal church in nearby Ventura to our liking. About this time, a dozen families in Camarillo organized to form an Episcopal church and Sunday School for our children. The Sunday School first met in the local VFW hall. Then we began church services in a chapel of the Griffin Funeral Home. When we outgrew the chapel, we met in the Women's Club in nearby town of Somis. By this time we had sufficient attendance that we received the support of the Bishop of the Diocese of Los Angeles to form St. Columba's Episcopal Church. I served on the Vestry and also as Junior Warden. St. Columba's was our family church as long as we lived in Camarillo. Later when we moved to Washington, DC, we joined St. Luke's Episcopal Church in Bethesda. We were active in St. Luke's and again I served on the Vestry and two terms as Senior Warden. After thirty years at St. Luke's, we moved our membership to St. Francis Episcopal Church in Potomac, Maryland, where we continue to worship.

Besides my work at Pt. Mugu, I was attending graduate classes at UCLA, driving the fifty miles down to Los Angeles two nights a week. After five years of this routine, I received my Masters Degree of Engineering from UCLA. One semester I taught a graduate course in servomechanisms for UCLA Extension.

My really big break came in 1959 when I was selected as the Navy's Sloan Fellow for a year's graduate study at MIT in Boston. By this time, we had a third child, Michael, who was two year's old. In June, 1959, Mary and I with our three children drove from California to Boston and I began a very interesting year of study in the Sloan School of Management at MIT. My Sloan classmates were forty-four successful middle-management types, mostly from industry. Our class included three foreigners: one from India, one from Egypt and another from England. The fact that I had been taking graduate courses and could discipline myself for study helped a lot to stay up with the heavy course load at MIT. The course of twelve months was intense, but very interesting, and led to a Masters Degree in Industrial Management. In addition, the year's stay in Boston, with all its history, was very enriching for the whole family.

We returned to California in the summer of 1960 and I was promoted to a new job as Deputy Head, Missile Programs Department at the Naval Missile Test Center. This job was different from those I had previously held in that it involved more management and less engineering. The Missile Programs Department had Program Officers for all of the missiles under test and evaluation at our base. In addition we were responsible for the planning and conduct of all of the flight tests of the missiles and their guidance systems, whether they were air launched or ship launched.

My Sloan Fellow course at MIT had been paid for by the Navy; in return, I was obligated to stay with the government for two additional years. In the spring of 1962, near the end of my two years of obligated service, I was encouraged by my friend Jack Van Ness to consider joining the National Aeronautics and Space Administration (NASA). Commander Jack Van Ness had been one of the Program Officers and Flight Test Pilots in our department at Pt. Mugu. After he was ordered from our base to the Navy Department in Washington, he was detailed to NASA, Manned Space Flight. This was the time of the buildup of NASA and the first manned space flights. NASA was augmenting their civilian force with selected officers from the Navy and the Air Force. These were exciting times in the space program; John Glenn had just completed the first orbital flight in Friendship 7 in February 1962.

Although I had no thoughts of leaving the Missile Test Center at the time, Jack convinced me that the next time I came to Washington I should at least talk to some of the NASA officials. I followed his advice and had an interview with George Low, Director, Spacecraft and Flight Missions in the Office of Manned Spaceflight, NASA Headquarters. George Low was responsible for the ongoing Mercury program as well as the development of the Gemini two-man spacecraft and its launch vehicle and the Apollo (Lunar) Spacecraft. I was very impressed by the NASA personnel, particularly George Low. NASA was a vibrant organization with personnel enthusiastically committed to the agency goals. I had several interviews and when I left I wondered what impression I had made and whether NASA might offer me a job.

I know Mary detected my enthusiasm for the NASA work when I returned home from Washington. I tried not to be too hopeful about the job prospect with NASA. However, a week after the interview with George Low I received a telegram from his office offering me the position of Chief, Gemini. I would report to Col. Dan McGee who had the Mercury and Gemini Programs under George Low. I was both surprised and very pleased. This was a great career promotion for me but it also involved tremendous family implications. It meant leaving our many friends and my coworkers and uprooting the children from their school and friends. We had one thing in our favor; we had just made a similar move across country when I went to MIT two years before and we knew it was feasible. However, this would be permanent. Mary and I discussed it at length before we presented it to the children for their reactions. Naturally, there was some objection from David and Jean, the two older children. But in the end, all agreed it would be an exciting change to be part of the new space age. I accepted the offer from NASA and we prepared to make the move to Washington, D.C.

The Space Race

Gemini

The Gemini Program was managed out of the Johnson Space Center (JSC), Houston. Originally Jim Chamberlin was the Program Manager; later Charles (Chuck) Mathews took over. Gemini was a two man spacecraft launched by a modified Air Force Titan II booster. It was a follow-on to the Mercury Program that had put John Glenn into orbit in February 1962. Gemini was a smaller program than the mammoth Apollo Program to send a man to the moon and return him safely. The primary objectives of the Gemini Program were to demonstrate long duration flight of fourteen days, and to develop rendezvous, docking and extravehicular (space walk) procedures for Apollo's flight to the moon. In the fall of 1963 Dr. George Mueller replaced Brainerd Holmes as Chief of Manned Space Flight in NASA Headquarters. A major reorganization followed and Mueller became the Associate Administrator for Manned Space Flight with the NASA Centers at Houston, Huntsville and Kennedy reporting to Mueller. Mueller reorganized the Gemini and Apollo Program Offices and I was appointed the Gemini Director of Tests under George Low. Shortly thereafter, Low transferred to the

Johnson Space Center, Houston, as Deputy Director under Robert Gilruth. Along with his other responsibilities, Mueller became the Acting Director, Gemini Program and I served as Acting Deputy Director. This gave me frequent contact with Mueller which had an important influence on positions I was offered later in my career with NASA. Furthermore, my position as Acting Deputy Director meant I handled most of the day-to-day management issues with Chuck Mathews, the Gemini Program Manager at Houston. This was valuable experience for me.

Mueller was anxious to accelerate the Gemini flight program for two reasons: first, to accomplish the technical objectives which were applicable to the Apollo Program and, second, to be able to transfer Gemini personnel who were needed for Apollo. To this end, in late 1964, I was assigned the task of determining if the schedules could be shortened so that Gemini could be launched every two months. With two men from my office, we met with all elements of the program and determined that with some schedule and facility changes it was feasible to accelerate the program and launch every sixty days. I presented my findings and recommendations to top management in January 1965. They were approved and phased into the program. The latter missions achieved the two month launch interval and the twelfth flight completed the program in November 1966. Despite budget and technical problems, Gemini accomplished all its objectives and made major contributions to the Apollo program. The rendezvous technique which was used later in the Lunar landing, the ability of the crew to function for fourteen days in space and to perform extravehicular activity outside the spacecraft—- all of these objectives were developed and demonstrated in the Gemini Program. It was an exciting program and I was proud to be a part of it.

I had the good fortune to be sent by NASA to present a paper on the successful Gemini Program to the XVIIth International Astronautical Congress in Madrid, Spain in the fall of 1966. Mary came with me on this trip. My paper was the first to be presented on the opening day of the conference. Dr. Charles "Chuck" Berry, the astronauts' doctor, and I agreed to operate the projector or each other's slides. We discovered that the NASA projector didn't have the correct plug for the Spanish electrical outlet so there was a scramble to get this corrected in time for me to go on stage. My anxiety was increased further when I heard that a member of the Spanish royal family would be in attendance. Sure enough, Prince Juan Carlos, heir apparent to the throne, and his wife, Princess Sofia, took a seat in the front row just opposite the lectern where I was to speak. Despite some nervousness of mine, the talk received a standing ovation. Prince Juan Carlos, later the King of Spain, was no doubt interested because he was a qualified military pilot. For me, this was a very satisfying conclusion to the Gemini Program.

Apollo

In the summer of 1966, a few months before the end of the Gemini Program, George Mueller transferred me to the Apollo Program as their Director of Tests in the Headquarters Program Office. My immediate boss became General Sam Phillips, Apollo Program Director. This took place at one of Mueller's Management Retreats which he held once or twice a year. This one was at Williamsburg, Virginia, and all the wives had also been invited. George Mueller was good at organizing special meetings which were a combination of work and play. He often included the wives which did much to improve the morale and engendered a sense of "family" to the Headquarters management team. The demands of the jobs included long hours and frequent travel to Houston, Cape Kennedy and Huntsville, Alabama, as well as contractor plants scattered across the country. Mueller was aware of the strains put on families and did what he could to include wives in briefings and management retreats.

Tragedy struck in January 1967 when fire swept through the Apollo spacecraft during a simulated countdown at Cape Kennedy killing all three astronauts: Virgil Grissom, Edward White and Roger Chaffee. After the accident, George Low replaced Joe Shea as Apollo Spacecraft Manager at Houston. What followed were investigations, personnel changes, tests to explain what had happened and why and finally redesign and more tests. It was a twenty-one month period of remorse, intense work and finally success. The spacecraft was extensively redesigned, including a new quick opening hatch, and was finally ready for flight as Apollo 7. Apollo 7, with astronauts Walter Schirra, Donn Eisele and Walter Cunningham, lifted off on October 11, 1968 for a successful eleven-day flight putting the Apollo Program back on course for its objective of landing a man on the moon.

The next major program milestone came with the launch of Apollo 8 on December 21, 1968 using the powerful Saturn V booster. This was a circumlunar flight with astronauts Frank Borman, James Lovell, Jr., and William Anders. These astronauts were the first men to view the backside of the moon as the spacecraft circled the moon. On December 24th, Christmas Eve, Frank Borman read verses from Genesis in the Bible and wished all on earth "goodnight, good luck, a Merry Christmas and God bless all of you—all of you on the good earth."

After spending 20 hours orbiting the moon, Apollo 8 returned safely on December 27, splashing down in the Pacific and was recovered by the U.S.S. Yorktown. The flight was a spectacular success with all mission objectives met and gave the program great confidence that a moon landing could be accomplished on schedule in the summer of 1969.

Apollo 9, launched in March 1969, was an earth orbital mission which proved out the complete Apollo spacecraft, including manned testing of the Lunar Module. The schedule called for only one more launch, a lunar orbital flight, before Apollo 11, the lunar landing mission planned for July 1969. It was a period of intense program activity. One afternoon in April 1969, George Mueller called me to his office and told me he was moving me from the Apollo Program to start up a new program called the Space Shuttle. I was completely surprised and had no idea what the new job entailed. What lay ahead were years of work on one of the most challenging programs in NASA.

Space Shuttle

That after-work meeting with George Mueller was certainly an eye-opener to me. At the time I was deeply immersed in setting up the Flight Readiness Review for the Apollo 10 flight which was only weeks away. I was the Director of Tests working for General Sam Phillips, Director, Apollo Program Office in NASA Headquarters. Dr. George Mueller, Associate Administrator for Manned Space Flight was Sam Phillips' boss. When I arrived at Mueller's office, he was writing a series of milestones on his blackboard and immediately launched into a litany of tasks that needed to be done in the planning for the "Space Shuttle."

At first I didn't realize how this affected me until he said, "This is what I want you to do, Roy."

He explained that he wanted me to head up a planning group that would develop a proposal for the Space Shuttle. I made excuses about my involvement in Apollo, but he insisted, and further said he wanted me to immediately take up this job.

I remember his words, " I want you over here working this job tomorrow morning." I had never changed jobs with a 12 hour notice! I brought my secretary, Jewel, over the next morning and began the task of recruiting engineers from the several NASA centers to form our task group. Our group was called the Space Shuttle Task Group and I was the Manager. Mueller had paved the way for me with the Manned Space Flight Directors: Bob Gilruth, Kurt Debus and Werner Von Braun. Even so, it was not easy to convince people, many of whom were involved with the upcoming flights of Apollo, to be detailed to Washington for a number of months. Of course, there was the satisfaction of working on a new program and within a week I had commitments of about forty good engineers and administrative people who formed the Space Shuttle Task Group.

Our task was daunting. We had to complete our proposal in thirty days and then negotiate it with the Air Force to arrive at a final set of requirements within the next thirty days. We met the Air Force deadline also by working at a furious pace. Several aerospace companies were conducting studies for NASA for a reuseable space vehicle and these helped in our work. Our proposal consisted of five volumes: Summary Report, Missions, Desired System Characteristics, Vehicle Configurations and Program Plans (costs and schedule estimates).

The Task Group completed its proposal by early July 1969. Because of my three years with the Apollo Program, George Mueller agreed that

I should go down to the Cape to witness the launching of Apollo 11, along with other NASA Headquarters personnel. This was the mission to land and return men from the moon. My wife and I watched the magnificent launch of the Saturn 5/Apollo from the spectator stands at the Cape. When I returned to Washington, I learned that Mueller had scheduled a Management Council meeting at Houston for 20 July, 1969, the scheduled date of the landing on the moon. This was typical Mueller style. He knew the Center Directors, Gilruth, von Braun and Debus, would be there at Mission Control to witness this historic event and that the time could also be spent discussing other issues. He asked me to give a presentation on the Space Shuttle planning. So, like most people, I remember where and what I was doing at the time of the landing on the moon; I was briefing Mueller's Management Council on plans for NASA's Space Shuttle.

The planning work of the Space Shuttle Task Group was only one part of a large effort within NASA to lay out what the agency foresaw as its program for the post-Apollo period. The other major planning activities centered on a Space Station, a Manned Mission to Mars and various unmanned scientific missions, both planetary and earth orbital. NASA submitted all of these proposals in the late summer of 1969 to the White House Space Task Group, headed by Vice President Spiro Agnew. These expansive plans were in sharp contrast to the declining NASA budget which President Nixon had ordered. The Shuttle was given priority in Vice President Agnew's Space Task Group Report over both the Space Station and the Manned Mars Mission but that had little impact in the face of the budget situation. NASA's reduced budget and concerns of Congress ruled against the Manned Mission to Mars. The Space Station suffered a blow when NASA had to cancel the Saturn V for budget reasons. The Saturn V was planned to be the vehicle to launch the modules of the Space Station. The Space Shuttle enjoyed wider support, although there were repeated attempts to cancel the program by Senators Proxmire and Mondale. White House appointed committees were also skeptical. Without a commitment from President Nixon to allow the Space Shuttle program to proceed, NASA was limited to studies, both inhouse and by aerospace contractors, during the years of 1970 and 1971.

In October 1970 NASA sent me to present a paper on the Space Shuttle studies to the International Astronautical Federation (IAF) at its annual meeting in Constance, Germany. The IAF held its week-long meeting at a different country each year. It was attended by representatives from all the countries that were involved or interested in space activities. At this time several European countries were interested in building some part of the Shuttle so there was considerable interest in my paper. My wife, Mary, and our thirteen year old son, Michael, were in the audience and they were amused when a Russian attendee stood up and took a picture every time I put up another illustration. I had mentioned at the start of my lecture that I had preprints available for everyone so there was no need for the Russian to photograph my slides. The Russians were always very secretive about their space program and I guess they just couldn't believe how open NASA was in discussing future plans.

As a part of this same trip I met with British Aerospace management in Bristol, England, and discussed their interest in being a part of the Shuttle development. They had proposed to build the vertical fin and furnish flight test instrumentation. In the final analysis, NASA decided not to involve any foreign contractors in the Space Shuttle development in a way which would be "mission critical." Thus the only involvements were Canada, with the Remote Manipulator, and the European Space Agency, which later built the Spacelab for experiments in the Shuttle payload bay.

In December 1970, the status of the program was upgraded from our Space Shuttle Task Group to the Space Shuttle Program Office and Charles Donlan was named the Director. He retained me as Deputy Director, Space Shuttle Program. I knew Donlan because he had been the Associate Administrator, Manned Space Flight. We quickly became friends and formed an excellent working relationship. Charlie, as I called him, had come to Washington from his position as Deputy Director, NASA Langley Research Center.

Until mid 1971 NASA had concentrated on a fully reuseable Shuttle which had a manned fly-back booster plus the orbiter. Although the fully reuseable vehicle promised lower cost per flight (because all the hardware was recovered), the development costs were high. By this time, decisions had been made to narrow the orbiter configuration to one with a delta wing and a payload bay size of 15 feet by 60 feet with a lift capacity of 65,000 pounds for due east launch from Cape Canaveral. These capabilities would accommodate large payloads (like the Hubble Space Telescope), synchronous orbit and planetary payloads with their upper rocket stages, future Space Station modules and the planned Air Force payloads. In addition, the delta wing configuration would provide a predictable aerodynamic and thermal flight through the hypersonic regime down to subsonic flight. Furthermore, the delta wing configuration would provide a cross-range of 1100 miles needed for a first orbit abort to the Edwards Air Force Base and satisfy the Air Force requirement for quick response missions.

However, in the fall of 1971 as the FY 72 budget was being established, the Office of Management and Budget (OMB), formerly Bureau of the Budget (BOB), pressured NASA into reexamining a series of configurations other than NASA's preferred fully reuseable Shuttle. The planned FY 72 budget for NASA would not accommodate the fully reuseable Shuttle. Those of us in the program office together with our study contractors conducted trade-off studies of smaller vehicles, a glider-orbiter launched atop an Air Force Titan III and the configuration with an external hydrogen-oxygen tank, two rocket boosters and the orbiter. We had studied the latter configuration during 1971 and understood its pros and cons. The negotiations between Dr. Jim Fletcher, NASA Administrator, and OMB personnel were intense with Dr. Fletcher refusing to allow OMB to dictate a Shuttle configuration and size that would not provide the needed capability. Finally, George Schultz, head of OMB, overruled his own people and recommended to President Nixon that the Space Shuttle Program be approved with the payload size and weight as recommended by NASA. The configuration agreed to was essentially what flies today: an orbiter with external tank and two parallel burning boosters. In a meeting with Dr. Fletcher at the

President's home in San Clemente, California on January 5, 1972, President Nixon gave the formal go-ahead to the Space Shuttle Program.

Having done more than two years of studies, NASA was now ready to contract for the development of the Shuttle. It had long been agreed that the two toughest parts of the development would be the Space Shuttle Main Engine (SSME) and the lightweight thermal protection system (TPS), called "tiles." NASA and Lockheed were already working on the TPS. By April 1972 Rocketdyne won the competition and began work on the Main Engine. Several months later in July 1972 Rockwell International won the competition for the orbiter over McDonnell and Grumman. However, Rockwell subcontracted about one half of the contract, including these major components:

Grumman - wing

McDonnell - onboard rocket maneuvering system

Fairchild - vertical fin

Convair - mid-fuselage (payload bay)

Contracts for the Solid Rocket Boosters (SRB) and the External Tank (ET) were not let until 1973. During this period NASA was under extreme budget pressure, so the contracts for the SRB and the ET were phased later in order to keep the annual expenditures as low as possible. Thiokol, located in Utah, was selected to build the SRB's; Martin would build the ET at NASA's Michoud Facility in Louisiana.

By 1973, all the major Orbiter configuration decisions had been decided except for the question of whether the Orbiter should have air breathing (jet) engines to provide a go-around capability for landing. Carrying the jet engines to orbit and back posed considerable technology questions and amounted to a significant reduction in payload. The NASA Flight Research Facility (FRC), adjoining the Edwards Air Force Base in California, argued forcefully that their experience with lifting body airplanes demonstrated that the Orbiter could successfully glide to its landing site without the need for a go-around capability. Hence no air breathing engines would be needed. Most pilots are wary of intentional dead-stick landings so the debate within the program and with the Air Force was spirited. Dave Scott, astronaut, was the Director of FRC at the time. He presented their past and current experience to NASA

Headquarters and urged all program management people to come out to FRC and take a flight in their Lockheed TF-104 which could fairly approximate the steep flight path of the Orbiter. I had known Dave Scott from the Gemini Program and agreed to make a flight in their two-place F-104 fighter. John Manke, FRC research pilot, took me up to thirty thousand feet to begin the simulated Orbiter descent. The glide slope of the TF-104 was approximately the same as the Orbiter under these conditions: jet engine at idle, landing gear down and speed brakes extended. With this configuration, we pushed over into a steep glide and aimed for a mark on the runway below. Although Manke made his landing flare a few feet high and didn't actually touch down on the runway, it was clear that he easily could have done so. A number of the future Space Shuttle astronauts and program people made flights in the TF-104 and were convinced that an Orbiter without go-around capability could safely land on the runway. In fact, flights in the TF-104 became a part of the astronaut training program. Later that year, the program made the decision that the Orbiter would have no air-breathing engines for go-around. Dead stick landings of the Orbiter throughout the program proved not to be a problem.

Both the Boeing 747 and the Lockheed C-5A were studied as possible planes which could transport the orbiter and serve as a launch platform for the forthcoming Approach and Landing Tests of the orbiter. After many studies and simulations, it was determined that with some modifications, the 747 would best serve NASA's need. This was a period when the nation's airlines had surplus planes, so NASA was able to purchase a used American Airlines 747 for $15 million dollars in June 1974. Boeing made the modifications to the 747 to allow it to carry and launch the orbiter.

By the end of 1973 all of the major elements of the Space Shuttle were in development. Dr. Myron (Mike) Malkin replaced Donlan as Director, Space Shuttle Program and I continued as Deputy Director. In 1974, John Yardley, former Vice President of McDonnell Douglas Aircraft, replaced Dale Myers as Associate Administrator of Manned Space Flight, NASA Headquarters. I had known Yardley since 1965 when he was the McDonnell manager for the Gemini spacecraft operations at Cape Kennedy. He was a sharp engineer and a good manager who guided the Shuttle Program for six years to its successful first orbital flight. I had the good fortune to work directly for him.

In 1974 Canada responded to Administrator Tom Paine's invitation of 1970 to participate in the Space Shuttle Program. Frank Thurston, Director of the National Aeronautic Establishment of Canada, made a proposal to NASA Headquarters for Canada to develop the Remote Manipulator System (RMS). This was the robotic arm which would allow the Shuttle to deploy and retrieve payloads as well as serve as a work platform for the astronauts while they were servicing a satellite in the Shuttle payload bay. Canada offered to fund the development, estimated at that time as $35 million, provided NASA agreed to pay for the production units to outfit the orbiters.

All of us who listened to Thurston's proposal thought it was interesting, but the question that remained was whether Canada's industry had the capability for such a unique technological task.

Jim Fletcher, NASA Administrator, directed that a team be sent up to Canada to evaluate their capability; I was appointed to head the team. In the fall of 1974, our team of people from Legal and International Affairs, NASA Headquarters, along with robotic experts from Johnson Space Center, Rockwell and MIT, spent a week in Canada visiting the companies involved. When we returned, I gave my report to the Administrator concluding that Canada had the capability to develop the RMS and recommended that NASA negotiate a Memorandum of Understanding (MOU) with them. In the spring of 1975 I led another team to negotiate the formal MOU with the Canadians. We held our sessions at Ottawa. The MOU was signed by both countries in July 1975. During this time there were considerable objections from several members of Congress and General Electric about the proposal to allow Canada to develop the RMS. NASA finally convinced those objecting that it was appropriate for the United States and Canada to collaborate on this program.

I continued as NASA's counterpart to Frank Thurston throughout the development of the RMS and made a number of trips to SPAR Aerospace, the prime contractor in Toronto, for technical meetings and design reviews. Frank Thurston and I resolved all issues at our level; none ever went to the NASA Administrator as happened on several international programs. The Canadian RMS flew on the second Space Shuttle mission and on nearly every one thereafter. It has had a remarkable record of utility and reliability greatly extending the mission capability of the Space Shuttle.

The Space Shuttle Program reached a major milestone in September 1976 with the roll-out of the first Orbiter, the Enterprise, at Rockwell's plant in Palmdale, California. Mike Malkin and I were there along with hundreds of others including lots of media personnel.

Mike and I were looking at the Enterprise with astronaut Fred Haise when Fred said, "You know, even with the unorthodox shape of the Orbiter, I still think it's kind of pretty and I bet she'll fly just fine."

A year later Fred Haise flew the first drop of the Enterprise off of the 747 airplane and successfully landed it on one of the runways at Edwards Air Force Base, California. I was there at Edwards Air Force Base along with thousands of others that cold morning in the desert for the first drop of the Enterprise from its 747 mother ship. The FRC pilots and astronauts Fred Haise and Gordon Fullerton had practiced every aspect of the operation along with Mission Control in Houston. This, combined with the many simulations and engineering analyses that had been done earlier, resulted in a safe and successful flight. The fears of some critics outside the program about the risk of this operation were not justified.

Manufacture of the Columbia, the first orbiter destined for orbital flight, was proceeding without major setbacks at Rockwell, as were the External Tank and Solid Rocket Programs. However, the two toughest development programs: the Thermal Protection System (TPS) and the Space Shuttle Main Engine (SSME), were clearly pacing the program with their problems. The TPS and the SSME had been predicted from the start as the two "toughest nuts to crack." The TPS primarily consisted of the light weight reuseable "tiles" which were bonded to the aluminum airframe of the orbiter. For the highest heat areas, such as the nose and the leading edges of the wings, molded reinforced carbon-carbon was used. The remarkable insulation properties of the fused silica tiles had been proven early in the program. Now, there was a need for a tougher surface coating. NASA's Ames Research Laboratory had two scientists, Howard Goldstein and Howard Larson, who worked with Lockheed and were responsible for an improved coating they called reaction-cured glass. Extensive testing of tile-structure components were conducted in hypersonic tunnels and arc jets throughout the U.S. But the most daunting part of the TPS program was the manufacture and installation of more than thirty thousand individual tiles, each one with a unique geometry. For example, on the lower surfaces of the orbiter, the tiles were six inches by six inches with a thickness that depended on that tile's location on the orbiter. Furthermore, the backside of each tile was shaped to match the contour of the orbiter skin at that location. In addition, each tile was bonded to the orbiter with close tolerances to its neighbor. The whole process was very labor intensive and time consuming.

When the Columbia was transported to Cape Kennedy atop the 747 airplane, there were many tiles yet to be installed. Furthermore, pull tests on individual tiles showed that the bond to the structure was not as strong as expected. To further complicate the situation, recent studies now predicted even higher airloads than had been the basis for the original pull tests. As a result, it was decided that each and every tile must be pull-tested after it had been installed on the orbiter and its strength had to exceed the expected airloads with a margin. The amount of work and time involved was enormous, but by summer of 1980 the tile situation was in hand. At that time the launch date for Columbia was set for March 1981.

The schedule for the first launch of Columbia had been revised several times: an early schedule had been 1979, then 1980 and finally March 1981. Schedule delays were due principally to three causes: (a) the tight budget which allowed little freedom to accommodate problems, (b) the difficulties with the manufacture, application and testing of the thermal protection tiles and (c) the problems encountered in developing the Space Shuttle Main Engine (SSME). The design requirements for the hydrogen-oxygen SSME were formidable. The chamber pressure of 3000 pounds per square inch (psi) was higher than any rocket engine ever developed. The engine had to be throttled so as to limit the ascent acceleration to 3 g's. It was computer controlled to provide automatic shutdown before a problem could result in catastrophic destruction of the engine. Each of the three engines on the orbiter had a rated thrust of 470,000 pounds. In addition, the SSME had to provide 109% of rated thrust for abort or maximum weight payloads. In addition to these performance requirements, the engine had to be reuseable with easily removable components. The development of the SSME clearly pushed the technology limits for rocket engines.

Rocketdyne, the SSME contractor, conducted engine component tests at their Santa Susanna Facility not far from their plant in Canoga Park, California on the outskirts of Los Angeles. Engine level tests were scheduled for the NASA facility at Michoud, Mississippi, where the Apollo Saturn engines had been tested. Numerous problems slowed the development. In February 1976 an oxygen turbopump failed on a test stand at Santa Susanna causing a fire which destroyed the complete test stand. Problems like this continued so that by September 1976, at the time of the Critical Design Review, the SSME had only run at 50% of rated thrust. However, things improved and by March 1977 an engine had run at 100% rated thrust for 80 seconds. A failure caused an engine fire at Michoud which slowed progress, but by August 1977 the engine had run at 100% rated thrust for 300 seconds - a milestone.

The continuing SSME test problems led the Senate to direct Robert Frosch, NASA Administrator (who followed Fletcher), to have the National Research Council evaluate the engine program. A committee of high level experts, chaired by Eugene Covert of MIT, set out to assess the program. I remember briefing the committee and also accompanying them on several of their field investigations. The principal conclusion of the Covert committee was that more component tests were needed before a full engine test was made. NASA and Rocketdyne responded to the Covert committee that because of the complicated interactions of the components with the other parts of the engine, the best way to test components, for example turbopumps, was to run them on an engine. The end result of the investigation was that Rocketdyne reactivated a stand at Santa Susanna, California in late 1978 and used another engine for component testing. This activity was in parallel to the engine testing at Michoud, Mississippi.

Meanwhile engine tests were going better in Mississippi. I was there in May 1978 for the first full duration (520 seconds) test of an engine at rated power. It was impressive with the thunderous noise and the clouds of steam from the cooling water enveloping the test stand. Later that summer I also witnessed a firing of 3 engines at once on a massive test stand that had earlier been used in the Apollo Program. Even with this encouraging progress, no engine had come close to running long enough without components being replaced. John Yardley, Associate Administrator for Manned Space and my boss, became concerned about the continued stream of changes. He wanted to fix the configuration and proceed to qualify the engines for flight. He sent very tough requirements to J.R. Thompson, SSME Project Manager, Marshall Space Flight Center. *The qualification tests were to be done on a single engine which was not planned to fly. Four mission duration tests which included abort simulation were to be run without any replacement of components. If a component was replaced, the entire test sequence was started again. In addition, Yardley set a requirement for 65,000 seconds of operation on a single engine prior to flight.* By the end of 1979, two engines had met the qualification for flight and a few months later an engine had accumulated the 65,000 seconds of running time.

The year 1980 produced continued progress with the tile installation and test on the Columbia as well as the qualification of the main engines for flight. All elements of the Space Shuttle program were sufficiently on schedule that the NASA Administrator wanted a firm date for the first flight. At a management meeting in the summer of 1980, the schedule for the first flight, STS-1, was set for the first quarter of 1981. All elements of the program were optimistic that such a schedule could be met.

After the complete Space Shuttle stack was moved out to the pad, a number of major checks were made. One major test was the Flight Readiness Firing (FRF). For the FRF, the vehicle is fueled, all systems are operating and the three main engines are fired for a short time. Of course, the solid rocket boosters are not ignited and the vehicle remains tied to the launch pad. Two weeks before the FRF, I attended the FRF Readiness Review at Cape Kennedy. It was attended by all levels of program management, both NASA and the contractors. Two weeks later the FRF took place on 21 February 1981. It was completely successful with all three main engines firing for 20 seconds. After this test there was high confidence that the first flight would take place in a matter of weeks.

The first flight of the Space Shuttle, Columbia, occurred on the morning of 12 April 1981 with astronauts John Young and Bob Crippen aboard. I was at a console in the Launch Control Center at Cape Kennedy and watched the Shuttle lift off from it's launching pad and climb into the sky trailing long plumes of solid booster flame. There was much cheering and back-slapping among the managers as the Shuttle rose in the sky. We were all celebrating the results of twelve long years of hard work since those early proposals of 1969 describing how we would design and build a "new reuseable space vehicle." After Columbia was safely in orbit, I flew to Houston and monitored the flight from Mission Control. Our next concern was the condition of the thermal protection tiles after Columbia's return from orbit. A number of us flew out to Edwards Air Force Base to await Columbia's landing. The crowd of spectators and media numbered in the thousands. After Columbia made a smooth landing and all systems were safed, we went out and inspected the tiles. There were a small number of tiles missing on the underside of the orbiter but no evidence of burn-through. Overall the flight was a success.

In September 1981 I was sent by NASA to deliver two papers on the Space Shuttle at the annual meeting of the International Astronautical Federation in Rome, Italy. My wife, Mary, accompanied me and it was particularly satisfying to be able to report on the successful first flight of the Shuttle. Eleven years before, I had presented our plans for developing the Space Shuttle to this same international organization; now I was able to present our success.

The second Space Shuttle flight, STS-2, was scheduled for November 1981. Astronauts Joe Engle and Richard Truly would fly. I was at the Cape again with Mary and experienced the launch with the tremendous roar of the solids and that long tail of fire like a comet. Mary, our daughter, Jean, and I planned to meet in Los Angeles and drive up to Edwards Air Force Base to witness the landing. The crowds were there as before and we saw the Shuttle high in the sky as it made its approach to landing. The landing was without incident and on inspection we found no tiles missing this time, an improvement over STS-1.

I had planned to retire from NASA after the second orbital flight of the Shuttle. So, after the launch I made the rounds in the Launch Control Center, stopping to congratulate all the Project Managers I had worked with over the years. Jim Odom, External Tank Project Manager from NASA Marshall Space Flight Center, and I struck up a conversation.

"Well, Roy, so you're finally going to hang it up, eh?" Jim smiled. "You know, things are looking pretty good about now. This is the second good launch we've had without any real significant snags. Seems like it might be good for you to hang around awhile and enjoy the fruits of your labors for a few more launches."

"You know, Jim, I figure a good time to leave is when everything is working good. No use waiting for some failure and then bailing out. This is the right time for me."

Endnotes

1. Based on CWSAC Battle Summaries of the American Battlefield Protection Program
2. Author's Note: The material contained in this Appendix consists largely of excerpts from the book by Jackson Day, Pastor, Grace United Methodist Church, Upperco, Maryland, James Day of Browningsville and his descendants: A Maryland Family, February, 1976, Columbia, Maryland. Rev. Jackson Day has generously given permission for me to use material from his book.
3. Day Genealogy File, Day Association Genealogical Committee, New York Public Library, APV (Day) 1916
4. Certification concerning the family name of Day, prepared under the authority of International Heraldic Institute, Ltd, Charlotte, N.C.
5. J. D. Warfield, <u>The Founders of Anne Arundel and Howard Counties,</u> Maryland. Baltimore, 1905, Regional Publishing Co., p. 5
6. Warfield, p. 7
7. Gust Skordas, ed., The Early Settlers of Maryland, from early land records of land given to immigrants to Maryland by sea, 1633-1680, Liber ABH, Folio 325. Baltimore, Genealogical Publishing Co., 1968, p. 128
8. Charles Francis Stein, A History of Calvert County, MD. Calvert County Historical Society, 1960, p. 255
9. Jane Baldwin, ed., Maryland Calendar of Wills, Baltimore, Genealogical Publishing Co., Vol. I, p. 211
10. Hester Dorsey Richardson, <u>Sidelights of Maryland History</u>, Tidewater Publications, Cambridge, Md., 1967, p. 289
11. Barbara Kaye Greenleaf, America Fever: The Story of American Immigration, New York, Mentor, 1974, p. 12

12. Greenleaf, p. 13
13. Skordas, p. 128. Liber Q, Folio 70
14. Skordas, p. 138. Liber 16, Folio 439
15. Baldwin, Vol II, p. 39
16. Mathew Page Anderson, <u>Tercentenary History of Maryland</u>, S. J. Clarke Publishing Co., Baltimore, 1925. Vol I, p. 268
17. Samuel Eliot Morison, The Oxford History of the American People. Mentor Books, 1972, p. 245.
18. Morison, p. 285.
19. Affidavit of James Day applying for pension, dated November 14, 1833. Original in National Archives—File designation James Day, Md W10713.
20. Morison, pp. 350-351.
21. James Day Family Bible, info copied in 1869. Original location unknown

Printed in the USA
CPSIA information can be obtained
at www.ICGtesting.com
CBHW031927090824
12961CB00009B/298